THIS IS
JEOPARDY!

CELEBRATING AMERICA'S FAVORITE QUIZ SHOW®

THIS IS JEOPARDY!®

CELEBRATING AMERICA'S FAVORITE QUIZ SHOW®

By Ray Richmond ★ Foreword by Alex Trebek

BARNES
&NOBLE
BOOKS
NEW YORK

Special thanks to Jeopardy! staff members Louis Eafalla and Bob Ettinger for their valuable assistance with this project.

Shortly before the publication of this book, Jeopardy!'s longest-serving writer, Steven Dorfman, who worked on the syndicated show for all of its first 20 years, died. This book is dedicated to Steven.

Tehabi Books developed, designed, and produced *This is Jeopardy! Celebrating America's Favorite Quiz Show* and has conceived and produced many award-winning books that are recognized for their strong literary and visual content. Tehabi works with national and international publishers, corporations, institutions, and nonprofit groups to identify, develop, and implement comprehensive publishing programs. Tehabi Books is located in San Diego, California. www.tehabi.com

President and Publisher: Chris Capen
Vice President of Operations: Sam Lewis
Vice President and Creative Director: Karla Olson
Director, Corporate Publishing: Chris Brimble

Senior Art Director: John Baxter
Production Artist: Mark Santos

Editor: Sarah Morgans

Proofreader: Lisa Wolff
Cover Illustrator: Gerard Huerta
Interior Illustrator: Scott Matthews

Library of Congress Cataloging-in-Publication Data

Richmond, Ray.
  This is Jeopardy! : celebrating America's favorite quiz show / by Ray Richmond ; foreword by Alex Trebek.—1st ed.
     p. cm.
  "A Tehabi book."
  ISBN 0-7607-5374-1 (alk. paper)
  1. Jeopardy (Television program) I. Title.
PN1992.77.J363R53 2004
791.45'72—dc22
                            2003027996

This edition published by Barnes & Noble, Inc., by arrangement with Tehabi Books
2004 Barnes & Noble Books

First Edition
M 10 9 8 7 6 5 4 3 2 1

ISBN 0-7607-5374-1

Paper-Durability Statement:
The paper used in this publication meets the minimum requirements of the American National Standard for Information Sciences — Permanence of Paper for Printed Library Materials, ANSI Z39.48-1992.

Printed in the United States

CONTENTS

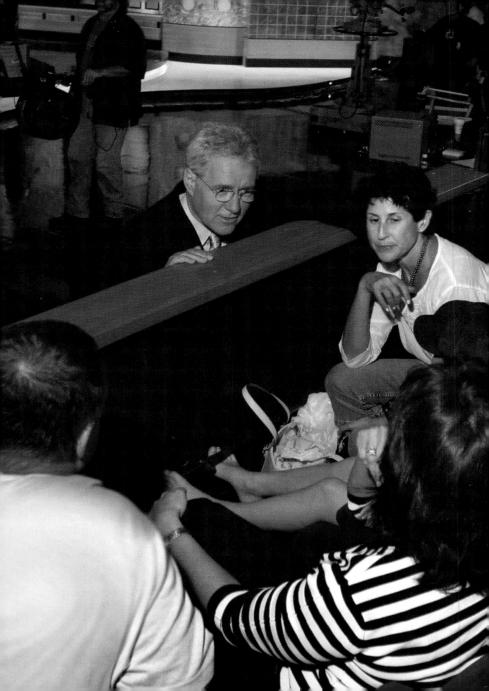

Twenty Years in the Blink of an Eye

We're thankful for our long-running success.
Foreword by Alex Trebek

Has it really been 20 years that this show has been on the air? If so, it has passed in the blink of an eye. The truth is that we at *Jeopardy!* are very fortunate to have been around as long as we have.

We're thankful that viewers have taken us into their hearts as they have taken us into their homes. We're part of their families. We're there every day. They spend a half-hour with us. There are clues for every member of the family so they can watch together as a family unit. And we're part of Americana. That's pretty special.

The secret to the show's longevity? Well, it's me, of course. Let's be honest. I'm it. No, seriously, the truth is that somebody else could do as good a job as I hosting the show. Hopefully, we won't get a chance to find out until I retire, and that isn't in my plans anytime soon.

People have asked what I'm really like off the show. I think that I'm just a regular, down-to-earth person. I fix sprinklers and repair plumbing and electrical. When I'm not taping the show, you'll find me puttering around the house doing stuff, fixing things.

Viewers have joined Alex, above, for a nightly round of *Jeopardy!* for the last 20 years. After Alex gets a full show under his belt, he likes to visit with audience members, left.

That may surprise some folks who figure that I might be into more intellectual pursuits. But you know, if you're a small-town boy, you're probably going to grow up to be a small-town man unless you have these wild and lofty ambitions of living the high life. That's not me. I have simple pleasures. I'm not flighty. I'm not an airhead. I'm not a nerd. I'm an ordinary guy, but I'm solid.

I still get excited hosting the show. It's the best part of my job. The most fun I have is the 30 minutes I spend with the contestants. We tape five shows a day, approximately six days a month. On each of those days, we'll have a production meeting and talk about all of the material. Then I get makeup, get dressed, go out and tape the shows, and I go home. It's about an 11-hour day.

Sure, it's a little bit long. But when people realize that I do it only two days a week, three weeks a month, they say, "Jeez, what a job you've got. How lucky can you be?" And they're right. I'm the luckiest guy in television.

When people want to know why *Jeopardy!* has been such a success and been around so many years, my theory is that Americans are very competitive and want some way to compare themselves to bright people. If they watch the show and come up with more correct responses than our contestants, they know they must be pretty bright. We have that great desire to evaluate ourselves compared to acknowledged intelligent people. And *Jeopardy!* gives them a chance to do that every day.

I'm very proud of what this show has been able to accomplish. We've been like this nice warm bath. You feel so comfortable with *Jeopardy!* And it is not known as a wild up-and-down show. There aren't these great highs and great lows. We just cruise along very smoothly. And now we've cruised to the 20-year mark, which is rather remarkable.

The fact that a show like *Jeopardy!* can sustain for 20 years is quite something because the TV medium as a whole keeps changing. We just keep chug-chug-chugging along and have remained true to our concept while introducing new elements and production values. It's still the same show today that it was in 1984, just in a slightly different costume. So, although we have evolved over the years we have remained true to our roots, and I think the fans appreciate that. When they tune in to us, they know what to expect. No surprises.

The book you're about to read is a marvelous celebration of 20 years of *Jeopardy!*, beautifully encapsulating what the show is and has represented. It sharply — and smartly — captures the sophistication, the playfulness, and the subtle evolution of a quiz show. I hope you'll agree that author Ray Richmond strikes the perfect tone of both wit and wisdom via a cornucopia of *Jeopardy!* notes, quotations, and anecdotes from our two decades of life. It's a fascinating read.

Enough with the preliminaries; let's get on with the show!

Wardrobe master Alan Mills assists Alex with getting into costume — invariably a well-tailored suit for the dapper host.

There's No Question About This Hit

Jeopardy! *has a living legacy of smart entertainment.*

It's safe to say that as *Jeopardy!* celebrates its 20th birthday as a weeknight phenomenon, there has never been a more popular quiz show in television history. Part of the reason for this is the fact that it is an ever-evolving beast, retaining its basic format while always tinkering with — and improving — the details.

Of course, at this point, *Jeopardy!* is no longer the mere title of a TV series. It is a genuine piece of Americana that is a living testament to the tireless passion and commitment of the staffers who keep it humming through 230 lively original episodes each season.

The show also remains an elegant monument to the sheer timelessness of what Merv Griffin and his former wife Julann created more than 40 years ago. When Merv and Julann came up with the concept for *Jeopardy!*, the tube was still reeling from the quiz show scandals of the 1950s, and credibility issues loomed for any producer looking to stick his toe back into those choppy waters.

But Merv longed to give it a shot, anyway. And when, on a plane flight in 1963, Julann suggested a game show

Alex uses a print-out of the clues, above, to keep track of the selected spots on the board. With another show complete, Senior Producer Rocky Schmidt and Executive Producer Harry Friedman prepare for the next one, left.

Announcer Johnny Gilbert has been warming up audiences and giving them the ground rules since 1984.

where contestants would be supplied the answers and be asked to come up with the questions, Merv sensed that this novel twist on the trivia format would be a winner. Before long, Merv was using the dining room of his New York City apartment as a run-through area while tweaking and refining what would become *Jeopardy!* He drafted close friends and relatives to serve as mock contestants. The original title of this creation was *What's the Question?*

Much pitching and testing and cajoling followed. A button-down fellow named Art Fleming was retained as host, and a renamed *Jeopardy!* premiered as part of NBC's daytime schedule on March 30, 1964. It would become a staple of the weekday television universe over the course of 11 years and 2,858 shows.

It was in 1984 that the *Jeopardy!* we know and love today arrived on the syndicated scene, distributed by King World. The irony is that, as Merv has noted with great glee, all of the research said it was a bad idea to bring back the show, that audiences didn't want another *Jeopardy!* — and certainly not at night. But Merv followed his gut rather than the advice of the so-called experts. And it's a good thing.

When the show returned to the air in 1984, it featured a Canadian-born fellow named Alex Trebek. Trebek had been a longtime game show host whose credits included such 1970s staples as *The Wizard of Odds* and *High Rollers*. His enlistment for *Jeopardy!* was an instance of the stars aligning perfectly — the right man in the right job at the right moment. The passage of time has further cemented the rightness of the choice. Indeed, it's difficult to imagine anyone else feeding contestants clues from that lectern.

When the show arrived on the scene in 1984, it updated the daytime show's card-pulling board system with a bank of video monitors and the dollar values were multiplied by ten. Merv used synthesizers to rerecord the famed theme music he had written for the show a few decades before. These updates helped distinguish the new *Jeopardy!* from the old and served notice that this wasn't your mama and daddy's *Jeopardy!* Well, on second thought, maybe it still was — just a bit slicker.

The show experienced its share of growing pains. During the first season, for instance, many TV stations throughout the country were unsure if the America of the 1980s was ready for a quiz show that required an honest-to-goodness brain. It ran in New York after midnight that first year and was similarly buried in other markets as well.

But distributor King World believed in the show and wasn't about to let it go without a fight. Stations were persistently lobbied to give *Jeopardy!* a shot in more advantageous time periods — and it worked. When WABC in New York began putting the program on in the early evening hours, the ratings soared and the show's reputation as a ratings powerhouse was sealed. At the same time, the fan base built to the point at which, today, it is the ultimate family show, one of the few shows that is embraced by every member of the household.

A few things have kept *Jeopardy!* at the top lo these many years. One is a refusal to compromise on the

Jeopardy!'s writers use thousands of reference materials, above, to create the clues. Alex reviews the scripts before taping begins, top.

THE ROAD TO JEOPARDY!

July 22, 1940
George Alexander Trebek is born in Sudbury, Ontario, Canada.

Early 1963
Merv Griffin's then-wife Julann has an idea for a "quiz show in reverse" during an airplane flight.

March 20, 1964
The original *Jeopardy!* premieres on NBC at 11:30 A.M., with Art Fleming as host.

May 21, 1992
Jerome Vered notches $34,000 to become the show's highest single-day winner, a record that will stand for more than 10 years.

January 15, 1990
New York City transit cop Frank Spangenberg obliterates the *Jeopardy!* five-day record with $102,597 in winnings.

October 1992
Celebrities compete on *Jeopardy!* to raise funds for charity in first celebrity shows.

September 1999
First Back to School Week has 10- to 12-year-olds competing.

November 26, 2001
Jeopardy! doubles the dollar values on the game board.

May 2002
Brad Rutter wins the *Jeopardy!* Million Dollar Masters Tournament.

May 15, 2002
Jeopardy! celebrates its 4000th episode at Radio City Music Hall in New York City.

The road to *Jeopardy!* has been somewhat of a Sunday drive, with fewer bumps and twists than many shows. If anything, it has been a trip with a steady incline, taking contestants and viewers to new heights each season. Here are some of the best-remembered milestones along the way.

January 3, 1975
The first edition of *Jeopardy!* has its final telecast after 2,858 shows.

October 4, 1985
Chuck Forrest sets *Jeopardy!* record, earning $72,800 over five shows.

September 10, 1984
The new syndicated *Jeopardy!* premieres, with Alex Trebek as host.

November 22, 1985
Jerry Frankel becomes the first *Jeopardy!* Tournament of Champions victor, taking home $100,000.

June 29, 1989
Alex Trebek wins his first Daytime Emmy Award as *Jeopardy!* host.

May 1989
Jeopardy! holds its first college championship — won by Tom Cubbage, a student at Southern Methodist University.

1987
Jeopardy! holds its first teen (February) and senior (May) tournaments.

April 16, 2003
Brian Weikle sets a five-day record by hauling in $149,200, breaking Frank Spangenberg's 13-year-old mark.

October 15, 2003
Sean Ryan becomes first six-time winner in *Jeopardy!* history.

January 13, 2004
Tom Walsh sets new earnings record of $184,900 in seven wins.

Each tape day Alex meets with the show's writers and producers to review the day's five games, above. Right: Discussions continue on the stage during the tapings, with the crew checking and rechecking the accuracy of responses.

difficulty of the game itself. It has never been dumbed-down, insisting instead on smarting-up even when the research indicated that the material should be softened. Another of the show's indispensable intangibles has been the creativity of the writing and research staff to consistently come up with clever categories like "Crimea River," "Lousy Scrabble Words," and "Doesn't Rhyme With Squat." The show has also been blessed with a stream of colorful contestants like Chuck Forrest, Eddie Timanus, Robin Carroll, and the unforgettable Frank Spangenberg, who have shown us that being smart doesn't have to be synonymous with being stiff and bland. These popular contestants are living examples of the magic that is *Jeopardy!*, of the mind, mouth, and thumb working together in glorious synchronization.

With a finger on the button to arm the contestants' ringing mechanisms, a judge prepares for playing to resume.

Jeopardy! has been parodied on *Saturday Night Live,* featured on *Cheers,* paid tribute to in countless films and TV shows as well as throughout the worlds of education and literature. It has given away more than $50 million while supplying nearly 300,000 clues over 20 seasons. Yet what has really distinguished *Jeopardy!* is the fact that it remains a nightly viewing habit for millions. It remains a mainstream standard by which the populace measures its own intelligence. That's clear from the nervousness that the *Jeopardy!* contestant coordinators report seeing when they go out into the world to recruit people for the show. A potential appearance is seen as a high point in one's life.

The *Jeopardy!* brain trust has not permitted the show to grow staid and stale even as the years pass. They up the ante by doubling the dollar values, or roll out a hot new set, or add the young and energetic Clue Crew to infuse the program with renewed zest and youthful exuberance. There are always the tournaments as well — of champions, college players, kids, teens, members of the armed forces, and celebrities. They're all part of the show's rich tradition.

What's perhaps most remarkable about *Jeopardy!* turning 20 years old in this incarnation is the fact that the show continues to be so ingrained in popular culture and America's consciousness. As the show moves forward, it

Two cameras keep an eye on the contestants from behind the set backdrop.

shows no sign of slowing down. Alex Trebek looks to have a few hundred thousand more clues in him at least. He will still likely be at the *Jeopardy!* helm when the Clue Crew members begin to creak a bit themselves.

This book is a celebration of all that is America's Favorite Quiz Show, with as much like-you're-really-there experience as can be offered in a book. It includes 400 Final Jeopardy! clues and responses — 20 apiece from each of the show's 20 seasons—that have been selected by the show's Emmy-winning team of writers. Accompanying them are 100 illustrated trivia items about *Jeopardy!* itself, embodying a wide and compelling array of facts and anecdotes (many culled from behind the scenes).

Each season of the show is introduced with tidbits of what occurred that year—both on the show and in the world. And in the book's final feature, would-be show contestants have an opportunity to find out if they're genuine *Jeopardy!* material by taking sample player quizzes

included in the back of the book. There is one for adults, one for teens, and a third for kids.

So prepare to revel in *Jeopardy!*-dom for the next 200-plus pages. You are about to experience what two decades of the show looks like in printed form. Who says that people who watch TV never read? After all, this . . . is. . . *Jeopardy!*

The control room staff, led by Director Kevin McCarthy (second from left) and supervised by Senior Producer Lisa Finneran (standing), monitors the onstage action.

A Contestant's Eye View of *Jeopardy!*

Admit it: You've wondered what it would be like to be on stage, ringing in to offer the correct response, coolly riffing with Alex after the first break, unveiling your perfectly strategic Final Jeopardy! wager to take the whole game. Even if you never make it onto the show, the following pages will offer a glimpse into what a Jeopardy! *contestant sees and does before the game.*

Contestants use telewriters for their names, Final Jeopardy! wagers, and Final Jeopardy! responses, above. Left: At the end of each show, Alex briefly discusses the games with the players.

Contestants are shown how to operate the buzzer, right, before they are given a run-through in a rehearsal game, top. Before their game, they stop off for some time in the make-up chair, above.

Contestants sign out with *Jeopardy!* staff, above, who accompany them everywhere — including lunch at the Sony Pictures Studios, top — before the big event, left.

Through the Ages

1984

1986

1988

1990

1992

1993

The shifts are barely perceptible: a slight widening or narrowing of the tie, a gradual increase of silver in the hair. Over the last two decades, *Jeopardy!* host Alex Trebek has maintained a consistently classic style, making the only dramatic change to his appearance when he shaved off his moustache during the 2001 season. Even the years seem to have treated him well — guess that's what happens when you not only have all the answers, but you know all the questions, too.

1995

1996

1998

2000

2001

2003

20 Seasons of *Jeopardy!* (and Counting…)

It started out with trips to the library, lots of typewriters, and only one computer for the whole office. But despite the changes in technology, each season of Jeopardy! *has had memorable moments, favorite champions, and fantastic clues. In this section we take each season in turn, summarizing the highlights of the year, offering some great on-screen and behind-the-scenes imagery, and including the producers' and writers' favorite Final Jeopardy! clues.*

Over 20 years the set has been updated and the equipment has changed, but the contestant's view of the board, above, and the presence of host Alex Trebek, left, remains the same.

IT'S THE YEAR that author George Orwell had warned us about. The term "Yuppie" is invented to describe young urban professionals. *Beverly Hills Cop* and *Ghostbusters* are riding high at the box office. *Dallas* and *Dynasty* are still packin' 'em in on TV along with a new family comedy starring Bill Cosby. A board game called Trivial Pursuit is sweeping the land. And a new take on one of television's most challenging quiz shows is just getting started in its latest incarnation, with Canadian native Alex Trebek serving as both its host and producer. The new *Jeopardy!* sports a computerized board, with dollar values from $100 to $1,000. It retains the popular we-give-the-answers, you-supply-the-questions format invented by Merv Griffin. Says Trebek of his role on the show: "I'm not to be considered an obstacle in any way, shape or form. If you ever wind up being an obstacle, the home audiences will turn against you because they relate to the contestant, not to you." The first season produces 15 five-time champions, a record that still stands into the show's 20th year.

**Biggest
One-Day Winner
and First Five-
Time Champion**
Elise Beraru of
Los Angeles, CA:
$23,800

**Biggest
Season Winner**
Paul Boymel of
Potomac, MD:
$56,200

**Number of
Five-Time
Winners**
15

The first syndicated *Jeopardy!* show aired September 10, 1984, with this line-up of contestants. Preceding page: A computerized game board has been Alex's on-air partner from the very beginning.

When *Jeopardy!* kicked off in 1984, the writers used typewriters and color-coded index cards to craft the clues and answers. The Internet was still in its infancy and wasn't used. The writers and researchers would troop down to the public library and look up newspapers on microfilm. There was only one computer for the entire staff, which housed the show's ever-growing database.

THE BIBLE

FIRST PERSON IN THE BIBLE TO BE IMPRISONED

AWARDS

IN 1950, MATHEMATICIAN BERTRAND RUSSELL WON THE NOBEL PRIZE IN THIS AREA

FAMOUS NAMES

IN 1974 THIS BASEBALL FIGURE SET THE RECORD FOR MOST LETTERS RECEIVED IN THE MAIL IN A YEAR, SOME 900,000

WORLD CAPITALS

BIRTHPLACE OF BEETHOVEN, IT HAS BEEN A CAPITAL ONLY SINCE 1949

THE OSCARS

FROM 1978-81, ALL OSCAR WINNERS FOR BEST SUPPORTING ACTRESS HAD THESE SAME INITIALS

HMMM

SSSHH!

WHO WAS JOSEPH?

WHAT IS LITERATURE?

WHO IS HENRY AARON?

1974 was the year he broke
Babe Ruth's home run record.

**WHAT IS BONN
(WEST GERMANY)?**

Update: The capital returned
to Berlin following the
reunification of Germany.

WHAT ARE M. S.?

Maggie Smith, 1978;
Meryl Streep, 1979;
Mary Steenburgen, 1980;
and Maureen Stapleton, 1981.

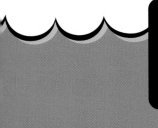

STATE CAPITALS

THE CLOSEST STATE CAPITAL TO THE NATION'S CAPITAL

U.S. STATES

THOUGH THIS STATE HAS NO RESERVATIONS, IT HAS THE LARGEST AMERICAN INDIAN POPULATION

LAND HO!

U.S. GOVERNMENT

HIGHEST ELECTED OFFICIAL WHO CAN SERVE AN UNLIMITED NO. OF TERMS

MEDICINE

IN 1806, FRANCE WAS 1ST MAJOR EUROPEAN COUNTRY TO FORBID THIS PROFESSION FROM PRACTICING SURGERY

TELEVISION

MT. VERNON, N.Y., NATIVE NOW HOSTS SHOWS ON ALL THREE MAJOR NETWORKS

When *Jeopardy!* premiered on September 10, 1984, the first clue selected was "Animals for $100." The clue: "These rodents first got to America by stowing away on ships." The correct response: "What are rats?"

WHAT IS ANNAPOLIS?

The capital of Maryland is only 33 miles east of Washington, D.C.

WHAT IS OKLAHOMA?

WHAT IS THE VICE PRESIDENT?

WHAT ARE BARBERS?

WHO IS DICK CLARK?

In 1984 he hosted *$25,000 Pyramid* on CBS, *TV's Bloopers and Practical Jokes* on NBC, and *American Bandstand* on ABC.

$0

$0

HISTORY

**IN 1952 IT BECAME
THE 3RD COUNTRY TO
TEST AN ATOMIC BOMB**

TITLED HEADS

**N.Y. FINANCIER
AL GRIMALDI IS NEXT
IN LINE FOR THE THRONE
OF THIS MEDITERRANEAN
PRINCIPALITY**

WORLD WAR I

**IT WAS THE
FIRST COUNTRY
TO DECLARE WAR**

THE THEATER

**BEFORE *A CHORUS LINE*
BROKE ITS RECORD IN 1983,
THIS MUSICAL HAD THE
LONGEST BROADWAY RUN**

THE MOON

**COUNTRY WHOSE
FLAG WAS 1ST TO
REACH THE MOON**

$0

Only three times in *Jeopardy!* history has a game ended without a champion because all three contestants wound up at $0. The first time was during the second broadcast of the show's maiden season back in 1984, when the three players each wagered their entire winnings on Final Jeopardy! and lost. It happened once again in season one, and it wouldn't happen again until the 14th season in 1998 — and hasn't happened again since.

WHAT IS GREAT BRITAIN?

WHAT IS MONACO?

Better known as Prince Albert, he used "Al Grimaldi" while working as a businessman.

WHAT IS AUSTRIA-HUNGARY?

WHAT IS *GREASE*?

Update: *A Chorus Line* has since been surpassed by *Cats,* among others.

WHAT IS RUSSIA?

Miniature Russian flags were scattered by *Luna 2* in 1959.

DAI
DOU

THE ZODIAC

THE ONLY SIGN OF THE ZODIAC NOT SYMBOLIZED BY A LIVING THING

NUMBER, PLEASE

NUMBER OF MOST RECENT YEAR THAT READS THE SAME WHEN TURNED UPSIDE DOWN

It's been asked why the *Jeopardy!* studio audience is prompted to applaud whenever the Daily Double appears on the game board. They are not, in fact, simply clapping for the Daily Double itself but the contestant's good fortune in landing on it. Only a small percentage of the time, however, does a successful player make it a true Daily Double, wagering enough to actually double his or her winnings.

FAMOUS FAMILIES

MEMBERS OF THIS ACTING FAMILY STARRED IN "GRAND HOTEL", THE "DR. KILDARE" FILMS, AND "E.T."

SHAKESPEARE

IN THE PLAY "JULIUS CAESAR", THIS CHARACTER HAS THE MOST LINES

THE FAR EAST

CITY THEN CALLED EDO, IN 18TH CENTURY IT WAS LARGER THAN ANY CITY IN EUROPE

WHAT IS LIBRA (SCALES)?

WHAT IS 1961?

WHO ARE THE BARRYMORES?

John and Lionel had roles
in *Grand Hotel*, Lionel
was in *Dr. Kildare*,
and Drew appeared in *E.T.*

I'LL TAKE
HOLIDAYS
FOR $500,
PLEASE.

WHO IS (MARCUS) BRUTUS?

The Final Jeopardy!
category on the first
syndicated *Jeopardy!*
broadcast was
"Holidays." The clue:
"The third Monday of
January starting in
1986." The correct
response: "What is
Martin Luther King
Day?" Greg Hopkins
won the first show with
$8,500.

WHAT IS TOKYO?

SEASON 2

1985–1986

$600

$800

$1000

A SUBTLE BUT SIGNIFICANT rule change on *Jeopardy!* allows contestants to buzz in only after host Alex Trebek has finished reading the clue, rather than upon its exposure. The alteration is made so players won't be forced to ring in before discerning whether they think they know the correct response. As a result, fewer contestants now submerge into a financial hole. Changes have also been made to the set to make it more dazzling and easier on the eye. After just a single season, *Jeopardy!* is the second highest–rated game show in first-run syndication. Promotional ads challenge viewers to "take the big-money risk" with "America's ultimate brain-bustin' trivia game." Chuck Forrest of Grand Blanc, Michigan, the season's biggest winner, shakes up his opponents by jumping around the game board and never allowing them to get comfortable with a category. It sets a strategic standard that would prove tough to match. The show holds its first Tournament of Champions featuring the 15 undefeated champs from season one in a two-week format invented by host and producer Alex Trebek. Meanwhile, a Nielsen survey finds that by the time children graduate high school, they will have spent more time in front of the TV than inside a classroom. Perhaps only *Jeopardy!* can save them.

Biggest Season Winner
Chuck Forrest of Grand Blanc, MI:
$72,800

First Tournament of Champions Winner
Jerry Frankel of Venice, CA:
$100,000

Biggest One-Day Winner
Harvey Becker of Venice, CA:
$25,400

Number of Five-Time Winners:
6

Alex proclaims the Final Jeopardy! winner on the jazzed-up second-season set. Preceding page: Alex relaxes during a commercial break.

The rules on a contestant's buzzing in changed following the 1984–85 season of *Jeopardy!*, during which contestants were allowed to buzz in as soon as the answer was exposed. It was altered to allow Alex Trebek to read the clues in their entirety before contestants could buzz in. Now, those who ring in too early are penalized 250 milliseconds (¼ second) each time they jump the gun.

THE CALENDAR

DATE OF THE FINAL DAY OF THE 20TH CENTURY

LANDMARKS

ACCORDING TO THE FAMOUS POEM, ITS NAME IS "MOTHER OF EXILES"

ART

TERM FOR THE WORK A CRAFTSMAN PRESENTED TO THE GUILD TO QUALIFY FOR A RAISE TO THE TOP RANK

CARTOONS

AFTER DEBUTING IN OPENING CREDITS OF A 1963 FILM, THIS CHARACTER GOT HIS OWN THEATRICAL CARTOON SERIES

THE 50 STATES

ITS TERRITORIAL CAPITAL UNTIL 1876 WAS VIRGINIA CITY; ITS CURRENT CAPITAL IS A WOMAN'S NAME, TOO

HELLO?

**WHAT IS
DECEMBER 31, 2000?**

**WHAT IS THE STATUE
OF LIBERTY?**

The poem is "The New
Colossus" by Emma Lazarus.

**WHAT IS
A MASTERPIECE?**

**WHO IS
THE PINK PANTHER?**

His debut was in the
Inspector Clouseau series.

WHAT IS MONTANA?

ARE YOU GOING
TO STAND THERE
THE WHOLE TIME?

WOMEN

FICTIONAL CHARACTERS

**MOTHER OF BONNIE BLUE,
SHE RAN A SAWMILL AFTER
THE CIVIL WAR**

20TH CENTURY

**TO HONOR HIM IN
1965, ELIZABETH II WAS
1ST REIGNING BRITISH
MONARCH TO ATTEND A
COMMONER'S FUNERAL**

ART

**THE TWO GEOMETRIC
SHAPES CONTAINING
DA VINCI'S FAMOUS
"VITRUVIAN MAN"**

YES.

U.S. GOVERNMENT

**THE ONLY ELECTED OFFICIAL
IN THE FED. GOVT. WITH DUTIES
IN BOTH THE EXECUTIVE
& LEGISLATIVE BRANCHES**

ENGINEERING

**20TH CENTURY ENGINEERING
FEAT WHOSE SLOGAN WAS
"THE LAND DIVIDED,
THE WORLD UNITED"**

Security is tight when you're a *Jeopardy!* contestant. The staff is duty-bound to prevent even the slightest appearance of wrong doing, owing to the quiz show scandals of the distant past. So players are discouraged from so much as winking at friends and family in the audience and can't walk anywhere unescorted. Once a player loses, the shackles are off, and he or she can go home.

WHO IS SCARLETT O'HARA?

WHO WAS (SIR WINSTON) CHURCHILL?

WHAT ARE A CIRCLE AND A SQUARE?

WHO IS THE VICE PRESIDENT?

WHAT IS THE PANAMA CANAL?

QUOTATIONS

IN THE CURRENT "BARTLETT'S QUOTATIONS", QUOTES FROM THIS SOURCE FILL 65 PAGES, MORE THAN ANY OTHER

EARLY AMERICA

FROM 1752 TO 1799, IT WAS STATE HOUSE FOR BOTH COLONY & STATE OF PENNSYLVANIA

THE OLD WEST

HE MADE THE LONGEST SINGLE RIDE—322 MILES— IN THE BRIEF HISTORY OF THE PONY EXPRESS

THE FLAG

PER U.S. FLAG CODE, ONLY PLACE IN U.S. WHERE ANOTHER FLAG MAY BE LEGALLY FLOWN HIGHER THAN OURS

GOVERNMENTS

COUNTRY WITH THE OLDEST WRITTEN CONSTITUTION STILL IN USE

The "think music" that accompanies Final Jeopardy! — written by show creator Merv Griffin — has grown so popular and is so embedded in the fabric of American culture that it can often be heard at baseball games during pitching changes and at football halftime college marching band performances.

WHO IS WILLIAM SHAKESPEARE?

Update: The current 17th edition contains 60 pages of Shakespeare. The Bible occupies 46 ½ pages.

WHAT IS INDEPENDENCE HALL?

WHO WAS WILLIAM "BUFFALO BILL" CODY?

WHAT IS U.N. HEADQUARTERS?

WHAT IS THE UNITED STATES?

MATHEMATICS

THE ONLY POSITIVE WHOLE NUMBER THAT IS THE SUM OF THE 2 WHOLE NUMBERS BEFORE IT

THE SUPREME COURT

THIS PRESIDENT APPOINTED MORE SUPREME COURT JUSTICES THAN ANY OTHER

IN THE NEWS

YEAR WHEN 1ST TEST-TUBE BABY WAS BORN, OSCAR TURNED 50, & JOHN PAUL II BECAME POPE

KINGS & QUEENS

ELEANOR OF AQUITAINE WAS ONLY WOMAN EVER TO BE MARRIED TO KINGS OF BOTH THESE COUNTRIES

LANDMARKS

THEY ARE AMERICA'S ONLY NATIONAL HISTORIC LANDMARK ON WHEELS

Although there has never been a three-way tie for a win on *Jeopardy!*, 45 co-champions have been crowned. Three players — Dane Garrett in Season 2, Sara Cox in Season 7, and Dan Girard in Season 14 — have held the co-champ title twice.

Jeopardy! Senior Producer Rocky Schmidt is the only show staffer who was also once a contestant. He originally appeared on the second season in the fall of 1985. Schmidt, then a lawyer, was a two-time champion, winning a total of $12,000. He was looking to change careers and wound up joining the show later that year as Alex Trebek's assistant. Believes Schmidt: "I'm the luckiest ex-contestant the show ever had."

WHAT IS 3?

WHO IS GEORGE WASHINGTON?

Washington created the court and appointed ten justices; F.D.R. appointed nine.

WHAT WAS 1978?

Jeopardy! staffer Rocky Schmidt won the game with this question.

WHAT ARE ENGLAND AND FRANCE?

WHAT ARE THE SAN FRANCISCO CABLE CARS?

JEOPARDY! AND *WHEEL OF FORTUNE* become the first game shows ever to be closed captioned for deaf and hearing-impaired viewers, a significant achievement. *Jeopardy!* also holds its first-ever Teen (open to ages 13 to 17) and Seniors (over age 50) Tournaments. The female population takes note as bachelor Alex Trebek declares, "I've been so busy with work that I don't have enough time to devote to a relationship. I'm getting to a point in my life now where I'm desirous of having a permanent relationship with somebody. It's just a question of freeing up some time and finding a person and spending some time with her." That ties in nicely with the new *Jeopardy!* ad campaign, which finds a swashbuckling Trebek rescuing damsels in distress with the message, "You put yourself in *Jeopardy!* for me! *Jeopardy!* is my life!" Back in the non-*Jeopardy!* world, everybody seems to be doing aerobics. "Baby On Board" signs are popping up in cars everywhere. Stephen King's *It* and Kitty Kelley's *His Way: The Unauthorized Biography of Frank Sinatra* dominate the bestseller lists, while in theaters *Top Gun* and *Crocodile Dundee* are ringing up big box-office receipts. And it costs $1.1 million to purchase a one-minute TV ad on the Super Bowl. Advertising on *Jeopardy!* costs somewhat less.

Alex saves a damsel in distress as part of *Jeopardy!*'s promotional campaign. Preceding page: *Jeopardy!* Senior Tournament contestants concentrate on the game board while Alex reads off the clues.

ACTORS & ROLES

IN A 3-YEAR PERIOD, 2 ACTORS WON OSCARS FOR PLAYING THIS CHARACTER IN DIFFERENT FILMS

AMERICAN LITERATURE

INSPIRATIONAL 19TH-CENTURY SONG FROM WHICH JOHN STEINBECK GOT THE TITLE "THE GRAPES OF WRATH"

FAMOUS WOMEN

WHEN SHE DIED ON JAN. 22, 1901, HENRY JAMES WROTE, "WE ALL FEEL A BIT MOTHERLESS TODAY"

20TH-CENTURY ELECTIONS

ONLY YEAR IN WHICH THE WINNER DEFEATED NOT ONLY THE INCUMBENT BUT THE PREVIOUS PRESIDENT, TOO

THE CIVIL WAR

THE SOUTHERNMOST POINT IN THE UNION WAS IN THIS STATE WEST OF THE MISSISSIPPI

There are more than 7,000 volumes in the *Jeopardy!* library covering every conceivable topic and specialty. It includes almanacs, encyclopedias, language dictionaries, cookbooks, biographies, novels, books of quotations, and travel guides. Among the volumes on hand: *The Complete Book of Cheese, Symbols of America, A Consumer's Dictionary of Cosmetic Ingredients, The Guinness Book of Marriage, The Vampire Encyclopedia, The New Cockatiel Handbook,* and *The Almanac of World Crime.*

WHO IS DON (VITO) CORLEONE?

Marlon Brando in *The Godfather* (1972) and Robert De Niro in *The Godfather, Part II* (1974)

WHAT IS "THE BATTLE HYMN OF THE REPUBLIC"?

WHO WAS QUEEN VICTORIA?

WHAT IS 1912?

Woodrow Wilson defeated William Taft, the sitting president, and Theodore Roosevelt, who had been president from 1901 to 1909 and ran on the Progressive ticket that year.

WHAT IS CALIFORNIA?

ELECTIONS

THE ONLY 2 PRESIDENTIAL CANDIDATES WHO HAVE WON 49 STATES IN AN ELECTION

POP MUSIC

THEY'RE THE ONLY FATHER-DAUGHTER PAIR TO HAVE HAD BILLBOARD #1 HITS BOTH INDIVIDUALLY & AS A DUET

When asked by Alex Trebek how he planned to spend his Tournament of Champions winnings, stamp dealer Marvin Shinkman quipped, "I think I'll lock myself in a vault with a large box of stamps, take off all of my clothes and roll around in 'em."

U.S. GOVERNMENT

IN 1971, THIS AGENCY LEFT THE CABINET & BECAME A NON-PROFIT CORPORATION

HIGHWAYS & BYWAYS

ITS ROUTE TODAY WOULD BE FROM THE CAPITAL TO CAPUA TO BENEVENTO TO TARANTO TO BRINDISI

ROYAL FAMILIES

IN 1932, THIS MIDEAST COUNTRY TOOK ON THE NAME OF ITS RULING FAMILY, WHICH STILL RULES TODAY

WHO ARE RONALD REAGAN AND RICHARD NIXON?

WHO ARE FRANK AND NANCY SINATRA?

Frank had many #1 hits; Nancy's chart-topper was "These Boots Are Made for Walkin'." Their duet was "Somethin' Stupid" in 1967.

WHAT IS THE U.S. POSTAL SERVICE?

WHAT IS THE APPIAN WAY?

WHAT IS SAUDI ARABIA?

HELLO?

MONARCHS

LAST 3 REIGNING MONARCHS
OF THIS EUROPEAN COUNTRY
HAVE ALL BEEN WOMEN

LANGUAGES

ONLY INDEPENDENT
WESTERN HEMISPHERE
COUNTRY BESIDES CANADA
WITH FRENCH AS AN
OFFICIAL LANGUAGE

SPORTS

THEY ARE THE ONLY
MAJOR LEAGUE BASEBALL
TEAM WHICH PRINTS THEIR
MEDIA GUIDE IN 2 LANGUAGES

FAMOUS QUOTES

IN 1946 IN MISSOURI,
CHURCHILL SAID, "FROM
STETTIN . . . TO TRIESTE,"
IT "HAS DESCENDED ACROSS
THE CONTINENT"

PRESIDENTS

1ST PRESIDENT WHO WAS
NOT BORN IN EITHER THE
ORIGINAL 13 COLONIES OR
THE ORIGINAL 13 STATES

Jeopardy! writer Debbie Griffin once rang up the office of Dr. Henry Heimlich to verify, for a clue, whether the doctor's famed Heimlich Maneuver was used for drowning victims as well as those who were choking. She wound up speaking on the phone to Dr. Heimlich himself, who confirmed that indeed his maneuver could be effectively applied for drowning.

WHAT IS THE NETHERLANDS?

Queens Wilhelmina, Juliana,
and Beatrix have all reigned
over the Netherlands.

WHAT IS HAITI?

**WHO ARE THE
MONTREAL EXPOS?**

They publish their media
guide in French and English.

**WHAT IS
"AN IRON CURTAIN"?**

**WHO WAS
ABRAHAM LINCOLN?**

DICTIONARY

WORLD BOOK

TIME

IT'S THE ONLY EAST COAST STATE THAT EXTENDS INTO THE CENTRAL TIME ZONE

WORD PLAY

"CRUCIVERBALIST" IS A 15-LETTER WORD FOR ONE WHO CONSTRUCTS THESE

FAMOUS AMERICANS

RENAISSANCE MAN, "HE SEIZED THE LIGHTNING FROM HEAVEN & THE SCEPTER FROM TYRANTS"

THE 50 STATES

THIS STATE, WHOSE FLAG FEATURES A BISON, ALSO HAS A TOWN FOUNDED BY & NAMED FOR BUFFALO BILL

ROYALTY

OF THE WIVES OF HENRY VIII, THE ONLY ONE WHO DIDN'T SHARE HER 1ST NAME WITH ANY OF THE OTHERS

Prospective contestants on *Jeopardy!* are given nothing to study in advance and no tips for playing. They are selected at random from the contestant pool by an outside agency before each show. Additionally, the categories and games are put together well in advance of each taping, without knowledge of or regard to which players will appear that day. Selection of particular games and the order in which they will tape are also made by the outside agency each tape morning. Contestants studying trivia as though cramming for an exam is not recommended, since the general knowledge parameters of the game are simply too vast.

WHAT IS FLORIDA?

WHAT ARE CROSSWORD PUZZLES?

WHO WAS BEN FRANKLIN?

When *Jeopardy!* host Alex Trebek is asked to recall the show's most memorable contestants, the list includes Dana Venator, who participated in the first Teen Tournament in 1987. Asked the most memorable aspect of the competition, Dana told Alex, "The hotel. We took pictures. And we're buying the robes." The accommodations remain one of the little-known *Jeopardy!* perks.

WHAT IS WYOMING?

Cody, Wyoming, is the city founded by Buffalo Bill and given his surname.

ME + MY ROBE

WHO WAS JANE (SEYMOUR)?

1987–1988

ALEX TREBEK — WHO RELINQUISHES his producer role this season while simultaneously taking on the hosting reins for *Classic Concentration* — exults that Frank Sinatra sent him a letter to say he's a fan of *Jeopardy!* Other fans now include Madonna and Billy Crystal as well. Adds Trebek: "This is the kind of show you're not embarrassed to admit you watch. Our message, if you can call it that, is that it's okay to be bright. I hope we're fostering the learning ethic in this country." Off the *Jeopardy!* set, the pooch Spuds MacKenzie is hawking Budweiser beer and Max Headroom is chugging down Coca-Cola. And a new *Jeopardy!* ad campaign aims to teach the populace "Jeopardese," which is described as "the ability to communicate in the form of a question." The season's Tournament of Champions winner, Bob Verini of New York, proves to be one of the most popular contestants in the show's brief history with his gunslinging, devil-may-care style and breezy sense of humor. He will endear himself with his steely nerves and dead-on impersonation of food queen Julia Child. Many years hence, Verini will return for the Million Dollar Masters Tournament and wager a true Daily Double in the finals that elicits gasps from the audience.

The cast of *Mama's Family* taped a show on the *Jeopardy!* set in November of 1987. Preceding page: Alex waits for a contestant's response.

WORLD GOVERNMENTS

THIS NATION'S 1936 & 1977 CONSTITUTIONS GUARANTEE ITS 15 POLITICAL DIVISIONS THE RIGHT TO SECEDE

RULERS

THE ONLY NAME SHARED BY 4 CONSECUTIVE KINGS OF ENGLAND

19TH-C. DEMOCRATS

HE SAID, "I AM THE LAST PRESIDENT OF THE UNITED STATES"

THE NEW TESTAMENT

NEVER MENTIONED BY NAME IN THE BIBLE, THIS DAUGHTER OF HERODIAS IS 1 OF THE MOST FAMOUS WOMEN IN IT

WORLD HISTORY

IRONICALLY, THE 1958 COMMUNIST CHINESE ECONOMIC DRIVE THAT FELL FLAT ON ITS FACE WAS CALLED THIS

It's often asked why the contestants finishing in second and third places during a particular *Jeopardy!* game don't get to keep their winnings. It's about maintaining good competition. Players might be tempted to play overly conservatively in the Final Jeopardy! round to protect their money. But that doesn't mean they go home empty handed: the second- and third-place finishers now take home $2,000 and $1,000, respectively.

WHAT IS THE U.S.S.R.?

WHAT IS GEORGE?

WHO WAS JAMES BUCHANAN?

President on the eve of the Civil War, he did not believe the Union would survive the impending crisis.

WHO IS SALOME?

She was given her name by Josephus, the Jewish historian.

WHAT IS THE GREAT LEAP FORWARD?

THE CATEGORY IS...
THINGS THAT HURT

THIS MUSICAL DRAMA WAS MADE IN 1927 & REMADE IN 1953 & 1980

JOHNNY CARSON BECAME PERMANENT HOST OF "THE TONIGHT SHOW" WHEN THIS MAN WAS U.S. PRESIDENT

IN A SONG FROM THE '30S MUSICAL "ROBERTA", THIS LINE FOLLOWS "WHEN A LOVELY FLAME DIES . . ."

One week Alex Trebek suffered from serious back problems and was on prescription medication while taping five shows. He was a bit off, failing to hit his marks and preside with his usual deftness and authority. But pro that Alex is, you still had to be paying close attention to notice anything was amiss.

THE 2 INHABITED CONTINENTS THAT HAVE NEVER HOSTED THE MODERN SUMMER GAMES

IT WAS THE FIRST SPOKEN WORD TRANSMITTED BY RADIO FROM THE SURFACE OF THE MOON

Senior champion Peggy Kennedy of Flushing, New York — who worked as a forensic toxicologist when she appeared on *Jeopardy!* — told host Alex Trebek that she worked only with the dead and assured him that "we won't have anything to do with you when you're alive." Quipped Alex: "You're not the first woman to have said that, believe me!"

WHAT IS *THE JAZZ SINGER*?

WHO WAS JOHN F. KENNEDY?

WHAT IS "SMOKE GETS IN YOUR EYES?"

WHAT ARE AFRICA AND SOUTH AMERICA?

This was true back in Season Four, and it's still true today.

WHAT IS "HOUSTON"?

Neil Armstrong said, "Houston, Tranquility Base here. The Eagle has landed."

RELIGIOUS HISTORY

BECAUSE FOUNDER GEORGE FOX TOLD A JUDGE TO "TREMBLE AT THE WORD OF THE LORD", HIS SECT WAS CALLED THIS

MAGAZINES

THIS MAGAZINE, PUBLISHED IN THE U.S., GOT ITS NAME FROM THE GREEK FOR "CITIZEN OF THE WORLD"

BODIES OF WATER

COUNTRY IN WHICH YOU'D HAVE TO BE TO BUILD A BRIDGE ON THE RIVER KWAI

BRITISH HISTORY

THE 1ST TUDOR MONARCH OF ENGLAND, HE WAS GRANDFATHER OF THE LAST TUDOR MONARCH, ELIZABETH I

THEATER

AFTER FINDING A NEW WAY TO MAKE THIS SOUND IN 1709, JOHN DENNIS ACCUSED ANOTHER PLAY OF STEALING IT

SORRY, NOT IF YOU WERE THE LAST MAN ALIVE.

WHO ARE THE QUAKERS?

WHAT IS *COSMOPOLITAN*?

YORICK,
WE'RE RICH

Some *Jeopardy!* champions use their cash windfall to pay off debts. Others take dream vacations or purchase their dream car. But Bob Verini had something different in mind. He used the money from his appearances and Tournament of Champions triumph to start his own theater company in New York.

WHAT IS THAILAND?

WHO WAS HENRY VII?

WHAT IS THUNDER?

This allegation is the origin of the phrase, "stealing someone's thunder."

AMERICAN POETRY

THIS VERB IS THE LAST WORD
IN ROBERT FROST'S POEM
"STOPPING BY WOODS ON
A SNOWY EVENING"

WOMEN'S RIGHTS

U.S. WOMEN FINALLY WON THE
RIGHT TO VOTE IN NATIONAL
ELECTIONS DURING THIS
PRESIDENT'S ADMINISTRATION

DECLARATION OF INDEPENDENCE

OF THE 56 PEOPLE TO SIGN
THE DECLARATION, THE
GREATEST NUMBER, 9,
REPRESENTED THIS STATE

THE 50 STATES

2 OF THE 4 STATES THAT
ARE OFFICIALLY CALLED
"COMMONWEALTH"S

MYTHOLOGY

THE FATHER OF KING MIDAS
WAS FAMOUS FOR THIS, WHICH
HE USED TO CONNECT HIS OX
CART'S POLE AND YOKE

Season four five-time champ Roy Holliday recalls recording *Jeopardy!* episodes every day for three weeks before his appearance on the show. "Then I'd stand in front of the set watching after dinner, since I knew I'd be standing on a podium in the studio. And I used a #2 Phillips screwdriver as my buzzer." Other contestants have simulated the buzzer using a ball-point pen or a cigarette lighter.

WHAT IS "SLEEP"?

The full line reads,
"And miles to go before I sleep."

**WHO WAS
WOODROW WILSON?**

The 19th Amendment,
passed in 1920, gave women
the right to vote.

WHAT IS PENNSYLVANIA?

**WHAT ARE VIRGINIA,
KENTUCKY, MASSACHUSETTS,
AND/ OR PENNSYLVANIA?**

WHAT IS THE GORDIAN KNOT?

Midas's father was named
Gordius or Gordus.

BZZZT

1988–1989

A COMPAQ 286 LAPTOP COMPUTER retails for $5,399, which means that the average *Jeopardy!* champ this season, earning $9,929.07, would be able to purchase nearly two with one show's winnings. *Rain Man* reigns at the box office, while *Roseanne* rules the roost on TV. In December, *Jeopardy!* passes the magic 1,000-episode mark, every last one of them hosted by Alex Trebek. The host also wins his first-ever Daytime Emmy Award. The show goes in search of players for its first Jeopardy! College Championship in the spring break hotbeds of Daytona Beach, Florida, and Palm Springs, California. Tom Cubbage — a student at Southern Methodist University in Dallas, Texas — wins the first college tourney, earning $26,600 in the process. This same year, 15-year-old Eric Newhouse of Iowa takes $28,100, becomes the youngest winner in the Teen Tournament, and earns the moniker of "powerhouse" from host Alex Trebek. Alex takes the contestant search team on a USO tour of Japan, South Korea, and the Philippines. Says Trebek: "We like to conduct these searches because we want to showcase the bright people who serve in our armed forces and bring a touch of America to them while on their tours of duty."

SEASON 5
IN REVIEW

Teen Tournament Winner
Eric Newhouse of Sioux City, IA:
$28,100

Biggest One-Day Winner
Garrett Simpson of Glendale, AZ:
$25,500

Biggest Season Winner
Brian Wangsgard of Redlands, CA:
$62,398

Number of Five-Time Winners
5

Alex has won three daytime Emmys for "Outstanding Game Show Host." Preceding page: Alex appeared with Ricky Scaggs at a USO performance in South Korea.

FICTIONAL CHARACTERS

"ALICE IN WONDERLAND" CHARACTER NAMED AFTER THE COUNTY IN WHICH LEWIS CARROLL WAS BORN

CHEMISTRY

CHEMICAL FORMULA FOR THE MOST ABUNDANT MOLECULE FOUND IN THE HUMAN BODY

PRESIDENTIAL ELECTIONS

HE WAS THE 1ST CANDIDATE TO RECEIVE HAWAII'S ELECTORAL VOTE

TELEVISION

IT WAS ON FOR 6 YEARS, GIVING IT THE LONGEST RUN OF ANY ANIMATED TV SHOW IN PRIME TIME

AMERICAN HISTORY

HISTORICALLY SIGNIFICANT EVENT OF JUNE 17, 1972

In the category "English Literature" during the fifth season of *Jeopardy!,* the clue was, "The longest word ever in the *London Times* crossword, 27 letters, was from his *Love's Labour's Lost.*" The answer: "Who was William Shakespeare?" The word: Honorifica-bilitudinitatibus.

HMMMMM A 27-LETTER WORD...

WHO IS CHESHIRE CAT?

WHAT IS H_2O?

WHO WAS JOHN F. KENNEDY?

WHAT IS *THE FLINTSTONES*?

Update: *The Flintstones'*
record was surpassed by
The Simpsons, which began its
fifteenth season in 2003.

**WHAT WAS THE
WATERGATE BREAK-IN?**

THE OSCARS

BRITISH ACTRESS WHO WON OSCARS FOR PLAYING SOUTHERN WOMEN IN 2 DIFFERENT FILMS

MONARCHS

IN HER WILL, SHE WROTE OF HER HOPE OF JUST RULE FOR THE INDIANS OF THE NEW WORLD

JEOPARDY!
JEOPARDY!
JEOPARDY!

AMERICAN LITERATURE

WHEN RIP VAN WINKLE FELL ASLEEP, THIS RULER'S PORTRAIT HUNG IN THE FRONT OF THE INN

ACADEMY AWARDS

THE 1ST PERSON TO WIN A SPECIAL OSCAR; HE WON IN 1929 FOR WRITING, ACTING, DIRECTING, & PRODUCING

MOVIE STARS

SHE MADE ONLY 11 HOLLYWOOD FILMS DURING HER BRIEF CAREER, CO-STARRING TWICE WITH BING CROSBY AND WINNING AN OSCAR

In the 1988 film *Rain Man*, Dustin Hoffman's autistic savant character Raymond Babbitt has an undeniable affinity for *Jeopardy!* He appears to watch the program incessantly, a practice the show's producers heartily endorse. Raymond actually says the name *Jeopardy!* six times in total, counting down "27 minutes to *Jeopardy!*" and "26 minutes to *Jeopardy!*" and finally "*Jeopardy!* at 5 o'clock."

WHO WAS VIVIEN LEIGH?

She received Best Actress awards for 1939's *Gone with the Wind* and for 1951's *A Streetcar Named Desire*.

WHO WAS ISABELLA (I)?

WHO IS KING GEORGE (III)?

When he woke up, George Washington's picture was hanging.

DAY 1

WHO WAS CHARLIE CHAPLIN?

DAY 3

WHO WAS GRACE KELLY?

HISTORY

AT THE REQUEST OF THE KING OF ENGLAND, POPE INNOCENT III ANNULLED THIS IN 1215

SOUTH AMERICA

THIS SOUTH AMERICAN COUNTRY IS NAMED FOR AN ITALIAN CITY

AMERICANA

IT WAS PUBLISHED ANNUALLY FROM 1732–57 & CREDITED TO AN IMAGINARY ASTRONOMER

MOVIES

TITLE OF A 1960 SPENCER TRACY FILM, IT COMPLETES THE BIBLICAL QUOTE, "HE THAT TROUBLETH HIS OWN HOUSE SHALL . . ."

FOREIGN PHRASES

THE GREEK EXPRESSION MEANING "PHILOSOPHY [IS] THE GUIDE OF LIFE" IS ABBREVIATED BY THESE 3 GREEK LETTERS

DAY 2

DAY 4

Jeopardy! is taped in groups of five shows a day. Contestants are told to bring three changes of clothes with them just in case they begin a championship run, since it might look odd to the home audience if a player kept showing up in the same outfit day after day. Before appearing, contestants also receive a letter detailing wardrobe suggestions.

WHAT IS THE MAGNA CARTA?

WHAT IS VENEZUELA?

The city was named
for Venice.

**WHAT WAS *POOR
RICHARD'S ALMANAC*?**

"Poor Richard" was
actually Ben Franklin.

WHAT IS *INHERIT THE WIND*?

**WHAT ARE
PHI BETA KAPPA?**

SEASON 5
FINAL JEOPARDY!

POETRY

IN A FAMOUS POEM, THE MONGOL EMPIRE SUMMER PALACE CALLED SHANGTU IS KNOWN AS THIS

CANADA

IN 1621 THIS CANADIAN PROVINCE WAS NAMED TO HONOR THE HOMELAND OF THE REIGNING KING, JAMES

THE CIVIL WAR

THE 2 UNION STATES THAT WERE INVADED BY GENERAL LEE'S CONFEDERATE ARMIES

INVENTORS

A UNIT USED TO MEASURE THE INTENSITY OF SOUND IS NAMED AFTER THIS INVENTOR

LANDMARKS

IRISH-BORN ARCHITECT JAMES HOBAN DESIGNED THIS BUILDING IN 1792 & FINISHED REBUILDING IT 25 YEARS LATER

When *Jeopardy!* conducted the first search for contestants in its inaugural college tournament, a tent was set up on the beach in Daytona Beach, Florida, during spring break. A coordinator would take to the bullhorn and announce, "*Jeopardy!* testing in ten minutes!" Vacationing students would approach, put down their beer cans, and try their hands at *Jeopardy!*

WHAT IS XANADU?

The poem was "Kubla Khan" by Samuel Taylor Coleridge.

WHAT IS NOVA SCOTIA?

"New Scotland" referred to the homeland of James I of England, who was also James VI of Scotland.

WHAT ARE MARYLAND AND PENNSYLVANIA?

WHO IS ALEXANDER GRAHAM BELL?

The decibel is the unit of measure.

WHAT IS THE WHITE HOUSE?

During its two decades on the air, *Jeopardy!* has won 24 Daytime Emmy Awards, which makes it easily the most honored game show in television history. No other show even comes close. It's a testament not only to the program's longevity and timeless appeal but also to the high regard in which the show is held by its TV community peers.

COLLEGE KID TOM CUBBAGE from SMU in Dallas proves that his College Tourney triumph of the season before was no fluke, winning the Tournament of Champions title. Later in the season, Frank Spangenberg, a New York City transit cop, sets the five-day record with more than $102,000 in winnings. The show, now promoted with the campaign "The most fun you can have with your brain," continues its commitment to the USO. *Jeopardy!* searches the world for great contestants by traveling to NATO bases in England, Germany, Belgium, and Italy. A prime-time comedy entitled *The Simpsons* premieres on Fox, becoming the first nighttime cartoon hit in a generation and later spawning a host of *Jeopardy!/Simpsons* tie-ins including *Simpsons* voice Dan Castellaneta's contribution to a "Readings From Homer" *Jeopardy!* category, a *Simpsons* storyline that finds Marge (Julie Kavner) as a contestant on the show, and a *Simpsons* home game.

Alex congratulates popular contestant Frank Spangenberg. Preceding page: Alex meets with U.S. airmen at Aviano Air Force Base in Italy.

Tournament of Champions Winner
Tom Cubbage of Bartlesville, OK:
$100,000

Biggest One-Day Winner
Frank Spangenberg of Flushing, NY:
$30,600

Biggest Season Winner
Frank Spangenberg of Flushing, NY:
$102,597

Number of Five-Time Winners
11

ENGLAND

**LEGEND SAYS
IF THE RAVENS EVER
LEAVE THIS HISTORIC
SITE ON THE THAMES,
ENGLAND WILL FALL**

SHAKESPEARE

**ACT I, SCENE III OF
THIS PLAY INVOLVES
A HEATED DISCUSSION
ABOUT 3,000 DUCATS**

THE CALENDAR

**THE 3 DAYS NAMED
AFTER A MYTHOLOGICAL
FATHER & 2 OF HIS SONS**

It was during the show's sixth season that Alex Trebek donned glasses for the first time for reading clues. "Yes, folks, it's that time of my life," he said.

13-LETTER WORDS

**WORD MEANING
"IMMEASURABLY SMALL";
ITS FIRST 8 LETTERS
ARE A WORD MEANING
"IMMEASURABLY GREAT"**

PRESIDENTIAL ELECTIONS

**IN 1988 NEVADA WAS THE
ONLY STATE TO OFFER THIS
CHOICE ON THE BALLOT,
& 6,934 PEOPLE TOOK IT**

WHAT IS THE TOWER OF LONDON?

WHAT IS *THE MERCHANT OF VENICE*?

WHAT ARE TUESDAY, WEDNESDAY, AND THURSDAY?

Tyr, Norse sky god; Woden, chief god of Norse pantheon; and Thor, Norse thunder god

WHAT IS INFINITESIMAL?

WHAT IS "NONE OF (THE) ABOVE"?

RRRR

TA DAA!

WORD ORIGINS

NAME FOR A FESTIVAL FROM THE ITALIAN MEANING "FAREWELL TO MEAT"

EXPLORATION

THIS COUNTRY'S FLAG WAS THE FIRST TO BE PLANTED AT THE SOUTH POLE

FAMOUS QUOTES

1 OF THE MOST FAMOUS QUESTIONS IN HISTORY, IT WAS ASKED IN 1871 IN THE VILLAGE OF UJIJI

A contestant in 1989 sang for host Alex Trebek the following lyrics he had penned for the famed *Jeopardy!* Think Music: "If you think your brain is strong, *Jeopardy!* will prove you wrong."

SHAKESPEAREAN TITLE CHARACTERS

HE IS INTRODUCED AS "THE TRIPLE PILLAR OF THE WORLD TRANSFORMED INTO A STRUMPET'S FOOL"

UGHHH!

U.S. STATES

IT'S THE ONLY LETTER NOT USED IN THE SPELLING OF THE 50 STATES

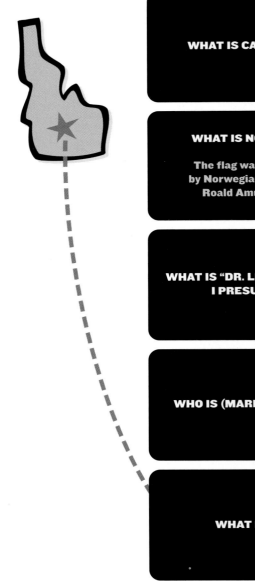

WHAT IS CARNIVAL?

WHAT IS NORWAY?

The flag was planted
by Norwegian explorer
Roald Amundsen.

**WHAT IS "DR. LIVINGSTONE,
I PRESUME"?**

WHO IS (MARK) ANTONY?

WHAT IS Q?

GEOGRAPHY

THE 2 INDEPENDENT SOUTH AMERICAN COUNTRIES NAMED AFTER FAMOUS MEN

AMERICAN HISTORY

HE WAS CAPTURED NEAR IRWINVILLE, GEORGIA, ON MAY 10, 1865

THE COMMONWEALTH OF NATIONS

IN TERMS OF AREA, IT'S THE LARGEST COUNTRY IN THE BRITISH COMMONWEALTH

One *Jeopardy!* broadcast in 1989 featured the following clue and response: "To get to Wallace, Idaho, from Boston, get on I-90 West, and the first one of these you 'hit,' you're there." Contestant: "What is a buffalo?" Correct response: "What is a traffic light?"

WORLD LEADERS

IN THE 20TH CENTURY THE BRITISH PRIME MINISTER WHO SERVED THE LONGEST

WORLD GEOGRAPHY

THE 2 NATIONS PLANNING TO BUILD A 10-MILE BRIDGE BETWEEN THEM TO LINK EUROPE TO AFRICA

**WHAT ARE BOLIVIA
AND COLOMBIA?**

The countries are named after
Simón Bolívar and Christopher
Columbus, respectively.

WHO WAS JEFFERSON DAVIS?

WHAT IS CANADA?

**WHO IS
MARGARET THATCHER?**

**WHAT ARE SPAIN
AND MOROCCO?**

PEOPLE AND PLACES

PLATO MENTIONED THIS PLACE IN "CRITAS & TIMAEUS", AND PEOPLE TODAY ARE STILL LOOKING FOR IT

GREEK MYTHOLOGY

IN GREEK MYTHOLOGY, SHE WAS THE 1ST WOMAN ON EARTH, & SHE BROUGHT MISERY TO THE HUMAN RACE

ACADEMY AWARDS

SUPPORTING ROLE WINNERS FOR 1973, THEY WERE 62 YEARS APART IN AGE & THEIR FILMS BOTH HAD "PAPER" IN THE TITLES

WILD WEST

IN 1879 ED SCHIEFFELIN FOUNDED A TOWN ON APACHE LAND IN ARIZONA AFTER BEING TOLD HE'D ONLY FIND THIS

MAN IN SPACE

AMERICA'S 1ST CIVILIAN IN SPACE

A partial list of the TV shows on which *Jeopardy!* has been featured: *Cheers, Beverly Hills 90210, Dave's World, Ellen, Frasier, The Golden Girls, The Oprah Winfrey Show, Saturday Night Live, Seinfeld, The Simpsons, The Tonight Show, Touched by an Angel,* and *Joan of Arcadia.*

WHAT IS ATLANTIS?

WHO WAS PANDORA?

WHO ARE TATUM O'NEAL AND JOHN HOUSEMAN?

O'Neal won for *Paper Moon* and Houseman for *The Paper Chase*.

WHAT WAS (HIS) TOMBSTONE?

WHO IS NEIL ARMSTRONG?

There have been four marriages over the years among *Jeopardy!* staff members who met on the show. Cupid fired his arrow for Marketing Director Annette Dimatos and Propmaster Jeff Schwartz; for Researcher Mark Gaberman and former Production Staff Member Heather Malcolm; for Promotions Manager Grant Loud and Writer Michele Silverman; and for Segment Production Supervisor Renee Rial and Camera Operator Ray Reynolds. The Reynoldses spent their honeymoon in Hawaii thanks to winning the trip at the staff holiday party.

THIS SEASON'S *JEOPARDY!* promotional campaign playfully asks, "Any Questions?" When it comes to this show, naturally, there are always plenty. There is no question, however, about the show's runaway popularity as America's favorite quiz show. *Jeopardy!* is now a household name, available on nearly 200 TV stations in the U.S. alone and in various incarnations the world over. Notes host Alex Trebek: "We came on the air very quietly, without any great fanfare. There were no fireworks, no bright lights, no wild and crazy music. We were just an easy show to get used to, an easygoing rhythm. That's served us well." It is also serving the school community as *Jeopardy!* receives several state proclamations saluting its educational merits and impact. The show's writers win a Daytime Emmy for the first time, underscoring the fact that writing and research form the *Jeopardy!* backbone. Movie fans are standing in line to see *Home Alone, Ghost, Dances with Wolves,* and *Pretty Woman.* On TV, *Cheers* — which later features its very own *Jeopardy!*-themed episode — ranks at the top. In fashion, hot pants and miniskirts are back in style, to the delight of grateful males from coast to coast.

Biggest Season Winner
Mark Born of Los Angeles, CA: $82,899

Teen Tournament Winner
Andy Westney of Atlanta, GA: $25,000

Tournament of Champions Winner
Bob Blake of Vancouver, B.C., Canada: $100,000

Number of Five-Time Winners
8

Jeopardy!'s writers won their first Daytime Emmy during the seventh season. Preceding page: Contestants rehearse on set prior to their appearance, using game material written for rehearsal purposes only.

AMERICAN HISTORY

THE ONLY 1 TO SIGN THE DECLARATION OF INDEP., 1778 ALLIANCE WITH FRANCE, PEACE TREATY WITH GREAT BRITAIN, & THE CONSTITUTION

LEGENDS

INCAN LEGEND SAYS A PRINCE NAMED THIS ESCAPED FROM HIS LAND & SET OUT IN A RAFT ACROSS THE PACIFIC

ACTRESSES

THIS ACTRESS WHO CO-WROTE 2 TRACY & HEPBURN FILMS WAS 88 WHEN SHE DIED IN 1985

MOVIE CLASSICS

THIS 1952 FILM WAS ADVERTISED WITH THE SLOGAN: "WHEN THE HANDS POINT UP . . . THE EXCITEMENT STARTS!"

LANDMARKS

THE INSCRIPTION ON THIS U.S. MONUMENT ENDS WITH THE WORDS "KNOWN BUT TO GOD"

Those who watch *Jeopardy!* will note that Alex Trebek appears to be writing something at his lectern. But he's not making his grocery list. Instead, Alex is crossing off boxes on the paper grid he has in front of him that matches the game board, so that he doesn't re-read a clue that's already been played.

TO DO LIST
- LAUNDRY
- PICK UP DINNER
- TRASH

WHO WAS
BENJAMIN FRANKLIN?

WHO WAS KON TIKI?

WHO WAS
RUTH GORDON?

WHAT IS *HIGH NOON*?

WHAT IS THE TOMB OF
THE UNKNOWN SOLIDER?

POETS

SHE WROTE "CATARINA TO CAMOENS," A POEM OF A PORTUGUESE WOMAN'S DEVOTION TO HER POET LOVER

ARTISTS

THE WOMAN IN HIS 1862 PAINTING "SYMPHONY IN WHITE, NO. 1" WAS HIS MISTRESS, JOANNA HIFFERNAN

COMPOSERS

HE ORIGINALLY TITLED HIS WORK "HOW PETYA OUTWITTED THE WOLF," BUT THAT GAVE AWAY THE END

MUSICIANS

THIS FAMED MUSICIAN DISAPPEARED ON DECEMBER 16, 1944, AND WAS NEVER FOUND

VICE PRESIDENTS

HE WAS THE LAST VICE PRESIDENT WHO DIDN'T SERVE A FULL 4-YEAR TERM

During its USO Tours, *Jeopardy!* has searched for contestants in England, Belgium, Germany, Italy, Japan, the Philippines, Guam, Spain, Greece, Turkey, Iceland, Scotland, the Azores, Bahrain, Bosnia, and Kuwait (among others).

WHO WAS ELIZABETH BARRETT BROWNING?

WHO WAS (JAMES MCNEILL) WHISTLER?

WHO WAS SERGEI PROKOFIEV?

Peter and the Wolf was the ultimate title.

YES!

WHO WAS (ALTON) GLENN MILLER?

WHO WAS NELSON ROCKEFELLER?

BROADWAY LYRICS

A JILTED LOVER ALMOST BREAKS A MAGIC SPELL BY RUNNING AWAY FROM A VILLAGE IN THIS 1947 MUSICAL

OSCAR-WINNING FILMS

THIS 1950 FILM WAS THE ONLY "BEST PICTURE" THAT FEATURED MARILYN MONROE; SHE PLAYED AN ACTRESS

THE CIVIL WAR

1 OF 2 STATES OF THE CONFEDERACY THAT DO NOT HAVE A SEACOAST

SPORTS

FOR THE 1ST HALF OF THIS CENTURY, IT WAS THE WESTERNMOST CITY REPRESENTED IN MAJOR LEAGUE BASEBALL

MEDICINE

COUNTRY IN WHICH THE FIRST SUCCESSFUL HUMAN HEART TRANSPLANT WAS PERFORMED

While Andre DuVoisin was a student at the University of New Orleans in 1991, the Metairie, Louisiana, native proposed marriage to his girlfriend on the air as he played in that year's Jeopardy! College Tournament. It was several weeks before the episode aired. But when it did, local news crews were on hand to capture Andre's girlfriend's response. Luckily, she said, "Yes!"

WHAT IS *BRIGADOON*?

WHAT IS *ALL ABOUT EVE*?

REACH
FOR THE
TOP

**WHAT IS TENNESSEE
OR ARKANSAS?**

WHAT IS ST. LOUIS?

**Update: San Francisco
now holds this distinction.**

WHAT IS SOUTH AFRICA?

THE
128,000
QUESTION

QUOTES

SOCRATES SAID THIS KIND OF "LIFE IS NOT WORTH LIVING"

FAMOUS NAMES

SOMETIME ON MAY 29, 1953, THIS NEW ZEALANDER HAD EVERYONE IN THE WORLD UNDER HIS FEET

FAMOUS AMERICANS

ONCE AN ILLINOIS LEGISLATOR, HE DEFENDED LEOPOLD & LOEB IN 1924

U.S. PRESIDENTS

HE WAS THE 1ST PRESIDENT TO VISIT MOSCOW WHILE IN OFFICE

BUSINESS AND INDUSTRY

WHEN THIS SOAP WAS 1ST MADE IN 1898, IT WAS NAMED FOR THE 2 OILS IT CONTAINED

Alex Trebek is now so closely identified with *Jeopardy!* that it's difficult to imagine him having had any job before it. In fact, he hosted numerous game shows before joining *Jeopardy!* in 1984. Alex's credits include *Reach for the Top* (1966–73), *Pick and Choose* (1971), *The Wizard of Odds* (1973–74), *High Rollers* (1974–80), *Double Dare* (1976–77), and *The $128,000 Question* (1977–78).

WHAT IS UNEXAMINED?

**WHO IS
EDMUND P. HILLARY?**

SHOW TIME!

**WHO WAS
CLARENCE DARROW?**

Only one time in memory has a would-be *Jeopardy!* contestant gotten cold feet and opted out of his appearance while waiting to go on during a taping day. As Senior Contestant Coordinator Susanne Thurber recalls, "The guy asked, 'Would it really screw you up if I didn't play?' We assured him that it wouldn't, that we had an extra person ready to go. He was just too nervous."

WHO WAS RICHARD NIXON?

WHAT IS PALMOLIVE?

JEOPARDY! **EARNS THE HIGHEST** ratings in its history while rolling out a brand-new, high-tech, state-of-the-art set that loses the carpet and incorporates a shimmering new floor, metal grids behind the contestants, and a refined host lectern. *Jeopardy!*'s ad now proclaims, "It's As Much Fun As You Think!" Jerome Vered of Studio City, California, becomes the show's highest single-day winner ever by notching $34,000, a record that will stand for more than ten years. Host Alex Trebek notes that *Jeopardy!* has now grown to become the standard against which all other quiz shows are measured. He offers, "Our viewers judge us by a much stricter rule. They expect *Jeopardy!* to be perfect in everything it presents by way of a clue. If the clues are going to be used on *Jeopardy!*, they had better be perfect." That same year, Elizabeth Taylor marries her eighth husband, Larry Fortensky. Author John Grisham's *The Firm* dominates the bestseller list. And Jay Leno succeeds the legendary Johnny Carson as host of *The Tonight Show*, with Carson's final show drawing a record 55 million viewers.

**Biggest
One-Day Winner**
Jerome Vered of
Studio City, CA:
$34,000

**Tournament
of Champions
Winner**
Jim Scott of
Columbia, MD:
$100,000

**Biggest
Season Winner**
Jerome Vered of
Studio City, CA:
$96,801

**Number of
Five-Time
Winners**
11

**Alex addresses
the contestants
on the show's
souped-up third
set. Preceding
page: Stage
Manager John
Lauderdale
observes players'
wagers for Final
Jeopardy!**

AMERICAN HISTORY

JOHN ALDEN WAS THE LAST SURVIVING SIGNER OF THIS

INVENTORS

ADVISED TO INVENT SOMETHING TO BE USED & THROWN AWAY, HE DID IN 1895 & MADE A FORTUNE

Few contestants are able to do what Jonathan Loeb managed during his eighth-season appearance on *Jeopardy!* During his interview segment with Alex, he actually played "The William Tell Overture" by tapping on his teeth. The host was duly impressed.

THE BRITISH EMPIRE

THIS COUNTRY, WHICH GAINED INDEPENDENCE IN 1981, WAS BRITAIN'S LAST COLONY ON THE MAINLAND OF THE AMERICAS

PRESIDENTIAL RELATIVES

HE'S THE GRANDSON OF ONE PRESIDENT & THE SON-IN-LAW OF ANOTHER

AMERICAN NOVELS

THE NARRATIVE IN THIS 1851 NOVEL CONTAINS A DISSERTATION ON CETOLOGY

**WHAT IS THE
MAYFLOWER COMPACT?**

**WHO IS (KING CAMP)
GILLETTE?**

He invented the disposable razor.

WHAT IS BELIZE?

WHO IS DAVID EISENHOWER?

David married Julie Nixon.

WHAT IS *MOBY-DICK*?

AFRICAN AMERICANS

IN 1978 SHE BECAME THE FIRST BLACK WOMAN HONORED ON A U.S. POSTAGE STAMP

ACTRESSES AND THEIR ROLES

THIS AMERICAN ACTRESS WON A 1960 TONY & A 1962 OSCAR FOR PLAYING THE SAME TEACHER

AMERICAN DRAMA

THIS 1938 PLAY'S 3 ACTS ARE TITLED "DAILY LIFE," "LOVE AND MARRIAGE," & "DEATH"

It was during the eighth season in 1991 that this exchange occurred on *Jeopardy!*: "George Bernard Shaw called this condition, 'The greatest of evils and the worst of crimes.'" Contestant: "What is marriage?"

THE NEW TESTAMENT

AT HIS MOTHER'S REQUEST, JESUS PERFORMED HIS FIRST MIRACLE IN PUBLIC AT THIS EVENT

ART

RODIN ORIGINALLY CONCEIVED "THE THINKER" AS A SEATED PORTRAIT OF THIS AUTHOR FOR "THE GATES OF HELL"

WHO WAS HARRIET TUBMAN?

WHO IS ANNE BANCROFT?

Bancroft won for playing Annie Sullivan in *The Miracle Worker*.

WHAT IS *OUR TOWN*?

Our Town was written by Thornton Wilder.

that reminds me of a story...

My food seems a little hot.

WHAT WAS A WEDDING (FEAST)?

WHO WAS DANTE?

FAMOUS WOMEN

**SHE WAS GRANTED
FREE USE OF THE MAILS IN
DECEMBER 1963**

MYTHS AND LEGENDS

**ONE LEGEND SAYS HE WAS
THE EARL OF HUNTINGDON &
LIVED FROM 1160 TO 1247**

FILMS OF THE '50S

**ONE OF THE 1ST LINES
IN THIS WILLIAM HOLDEN
FILM IS "THE POOR DOPE.
HE ALWAYS WANTED A POOL."**

RELIGION

**MUHAMMAD & HIS
FOLLOWERS FIRST
TURNED TO PRAY TOWARD
THIS CITY, NOT MECCA**

ANCIENT ROME

**PROFESSION OF THOSE
WHO SAID, "AVE, CAESAR,
MORITURI TE SALUTANT"**

Alex Trebek notes that if he couldn't have been an actor (or a game show host), he would have wanted to be a teacher, a politician, or a psychiatrist. And if he could have a fantasy dinner party, he would invite Joan of Arc, Mark Twain, Ava Gardner, and Alexander the Great.

mmmphh

HEY!!!

105

WHO WAS JACQUELINE KENNEDY (ONASSIS)?

WHO IS ROBIN HOOD?

WHAT IS *SUNSET BOULEVARD*?

After a taping Alex Trebek immediately changes out of his suit. The *Jeopardy!* host tends to be ultra casual when off the set, preferring to knock around in blue jeans, T-shirt, and sneakers and often getting around in a less-than-new pickup truck.

WHAT IS JERUSALEM?

WHAT WAS GLADIATOR?

The quotation translates to "Hail, Caesar, we who are about to die salute you."

U.S. PRESIDENTS

HE WAS THE ONLY SITTING
VICE PRESIDENT TO DEFEAT
A SITTING PRESIDENT IN
AN ELECTION

SPORTS

IN THE 1970S & 1980S,
OVER HALF THE LITTLE
LEAGUE WORLD SERIES
CHAMPIONS CAME
FROM THIS ISLAND

AMERICAN REVOLUTION

1 OF THE ONLY 2 PATRIOTS
NOT OFFERED AMNESTY BY
THE BRITISH IN 1775

AHHH

SHAKESPEAREAN CHARACTERS

THE 3 CHARACTERS WHO
DIE IN THE LAST SCENE OF
"ROMEO AND JULIET"
ARE ROMEO, JULIET,
& THIS PERSON

FOOD AND DRINK

BEFORE THE INTRODUCTION
OF DIET COKE, THIS WAS
THE LEADING DIET SOFT
DRINK IN THE U.S.

WHO WAS THOMAS JEFFERSON?

WHAT IS TAIWAN?

Jeopardy!'s host is the first to admit that he isn't quite as young as he used to be. But it was still a bit jarring for him when, in 1991, a contestant responded to the clue, "Born in India in 1847" with "Who is Alex Trebek?"

WHO WAS SAMUEL ADAMS OR JOHN HANCOCK?

WHO IS PARIS?

WHAT IS TAB?

JEOPARDY! **HOLDS ITS FIRST** Celebrity *Jeopardy!* competition, featuring such stars as Carol Burnett, Regis Philbin, Beau Bridges, Robert Guillaume, Ed Begley Jr., Emma Samms, Luke Perry, and Donna Mills competing for various charities. Cheech Marin of *Cheech and Chong* fame emerges as the week's high scorer. Philbin, meanwhile, jokes during his appearance that his buzzer doesn't work. This leads to host Alex Trebek's presenting Regis with a bronzed buzzer on *Live With Regis & Kathie Lee*. Being on the show isn't as easy as it looks. But Trebek believes that's a good thing. "If we were to dummy [the show] down, you'd get tired of it very quickly," he says. "Overall, the perception is that *Jeopardy!* is a tough show and it is. We're informative, educational, and entertaining." This season, *Jeopardy!* invites viewers to "Take the Challenge" and now airs in 15 foreign territories including Australia, Belgium, Canada, France, Germany, and Saudi Arabia. For the first time this year, consumers are able to stand their toothpaste up on end rather than squeeze it from a tube thanks to the release of toothpaste pumps. Disney's *Aladdin* rules the box office.

**Celebrity
Tournament
Winner**
Cheech Marin
$25,000

**Teen Tournament
Winner**
Fraser Woodford of
Lexington, KY:
$28,999

**Biggest
Season Winner**
Ed Schiffer of
Santa Monica, CA:
$65,903

**Number of
Five-Time
Winners**
7

**Alex meets with
Philippe Risoli,
host of the French
version of *Jeopardy!*
Preceding page:
Alex comes out from
behind his lectern
to interview the
contestants.**

THE CALENDAR

THIS RELIGION'S CALENDAR DATES FROM 622 A.D.

MILITARY LEADERS

THIS U.S. GENERAL WAS BORN APRIL 5, 1937, TO PARENTS WHO HAD EMIGRATED FROM JAMAICA

MUSEUMS

THIS U.S. CITY IS THE HOME OF A PERMANENT HISTORICAL EXHIBIT CALLED "THE SIXTH FLOOR"

ENGLISH LITERATURE

IN THIS 1653 WORK, PISCATOR TRIES TO CONVINCE VENATOR, A HUNTER, THAT FISHING IS A BETTER SPORT

JOURNALISM

THE ORIGINS OF THIS GO BACK TO 6 PAPERS THAT COMBINED TO TELEGRAPH NEWS FROM BOSTON TO NYC

Many *Jeopardy!* champions say that key to their success was staying relaxed, which helped keep the correct responses flowing. One contestant, though, decided that downing a dozen cups of coffee minutes before airtime was the way to go. No word on whether anything was flowing during that game.

WHAT IS ISLAM?

622 A.D. was the year of Muhammad's flight from Mecca to Medina.

According to *Jeopardy!* writer Billy Wisse, the time required to research a typical clue for the show is fairly standard. It boils down to roughly one hour per clue and, thus, five hours for each category. There are exceptions, of course. Some information and confirmations take considerably longer. But an hour for each clue is a good rule of thumb.

WHO IS COLIN POWELL?

WHAT IS DALLAS?

The collection is located in the former Texas schoolbook depository from which President Kennedy was shot.

WHAT IS *THE COMPLEAT ANGLER*?

The Compleat Angler was written by Izaak Walton.

WHAT IS THE ASSOCIATED PRESS?

HISTORIC NAMES

FOR HIS LICENTIOUS BEHAVIOR, MONK GRIGORI YEFIMOVICH NOVYKH EARNED THIS NICKNAME MEANING "DEBAUCHED ONE"

THE NOBEL PRIZE

THE CATEGORY IN WHICH THE U.S. HAS WON THE FEWEST MEDALS: 10

VICE PRESIDENTS

HE SERVED AS VICE PRESIDENT FOR THE SHORTEST LENGTH OF TIME, 1 MONTH

WORD ORIGINS

THE NAME OF THIS SWIFT CURRENT BETWEEN 2 OF THE LOFOTEN ISLANDS OFF NORWAY HAS COME TO REFER TO ANY WHIRLPOOL

CHRONOLOGY

DIONYSIUS EXIGUUS, A MONK IN ROME, IS CREDITED WITH INSPIRING THE USE OF THESE 2 ABBREVIATIONS

WHAT IS RASPUTIN?

WHAT IS LITERATURE?

Update: With Toni Morrison's award in 1993, the U.S. total has increased to 11.

Jeopardy! writer Billy Wisse was once obliged to call up the inventor of kitty litter to research a clue. He managed to track down Edward Lowe in Cassopolis, Michigan, and Lowe confirmed the story of how he realized that his grease-absorbing mixture might work well in cat boxes and began marketing it for that purpose.

WHO WAS JOHN TYLER?

WHAT IS MAELSTROM?

WHAT ARE B.C. AND A.D.?

FAMOUS NAMES

THE LAST OF HIS
56 CHILDREN, MABEL
SANBORN, DIED IN
1950 AT AGE 87

ROMAN EMPERORS

IN 54 A.D., AS THE
RESULT OF HIS MOTHER'S
SCHEMING, HE BECAME THE
FIRST TEENAGE EMPEROR OF
ROME AT AGE 16

LANGUAGES

SWAHILI CONTAINS MANY
WORDS BORROWED FROM
THIS LANGUAGE, INCLUDING
THE WORD "SWAHILI"

FAMOUS STRUCTURES

PRIOR TO THE COMPLETION
OF THE EIFFEL TOWER,
THIS U.S. STRUCTURE WAS
THE WORLD'S TALLEST

THE OSCARS

IN 1992 JOHN SINGLETON
REPLACED THIS 1941 NOMINEE
AS THE YOUNGEST DIRECTOR
NOMINATED

WHO WAS BRIGHAM YOUNG?

WHO WAS NERO?

WHAT IS ARABIC?

WHAT IS THE WASHINGTON MONUMENT?

WHO WAS ORSON WELLES?

FAMILIAR PHRASES

IN ENGLAND, IT WAS A PLACE SET ASIDE AT BALLS WHERE SERVANTS WOULD ATTEND TO PEOPLE'S WIGS

SPORTING EVENTS

IN 1911 IT TOOK 6 HOURS, 42 MINUTES TO WIN THE EVENT; IN 1991, 2 HOURS, 50 MINUTES

U.S. ELECTIONS

HE'S BEEN ON THE REPUBLICAN NATIONAL TICKET MORE THAN ANYONE ELSE — 5 TIMES

The contestants who are playing Final Jeopardy! hear the Think Music in studio just as viewers do at home. While some may think it a distraction, players typically cite it as providing an audible cue that signals how much time they have left . . . especially when it comes down to the final three beats.

NATURE

ABOUT 1,250 MILES LONG, IT'S THE LARGEST STRUCTURE EVER FORMED BY CREATURES OTHER THAN MAN

SPORTS

HE'S THE ONLY MAN VOTED NBA MVP UNDER TWO COMPLETELY DIFFERENT NAMES

Since the Jeopardy! College Tournament began in 1989, there have been no repeat winners among those colleges represented. The list includes Southern Methodist University, Rutgers, Georgia Tech, William & Mary, Grinnell College, Brigham Young University, University of Oklahoma, University of Arkansas, University of Michigan, Harvey Mudd College, University of Chicago, Drew University, Loyola University Chicago, Stanford, Texas A & M, and Middlebury College.

WHAT IS THE POWDER ROOM?

WHAT IS THE INDIANAPOLIS 500?

WHO IS RICHARD NIXON?

WHAT IS THE GREAT BARRIER REEF?

WHO IS KAREEM ABDUL-JABBAR (LEW ALCINDOR)?

1993–1994

THE SHOW CELEBRATES the culmination of its first decade. New York cop and longtime *Jeopardy!* favorite Frank Spangenberg admits during the show's 10th Anniversary Tournament (which he wins with $41,800) that being on the show has wreaked havoc with his undercover law enforcement career even as it padded his bank account. The second Celebrity Jeopardy! Week finds Jerry Orbach of *Law & Order* earning $34,000 for the Bide-a-Wee Home Association as the week's highest scorer. Leslie Nielsen, Kelsey Grammer, Pat Sajak, Paula Poundstone, Teri Garr, Sinbad, Tim Daly, Ed Asner, and Harry Anderson also are featured. The show has now amassed 11 Daytime Emmys all told and won the Outstanding Game Show prize four years running. Australia, Belgium, Germany, Hungary, New Zealand, Sweden, and the United Kingdom now produce their own versions of *Jeopardy!* Original episodes of the American show also run in 11 foreign countries. In theaters, *Jurassic Park* is scaring up big business. The Tim Allen comedy *Home Improvement* rules the airwaves, while bookstores are selling out of Robert James Waller's *The Bridges of Madison County* and Rush Limbaugh's *See, I Told You So*. Host Alex Trebek believes that books and his show go hand-in-hand. He says, "If watching Jeopardy! arouses a certain amount of curiosity about a particular subject, maybe people will pick up a book and read about it."

In the early seasons of *Jeopardy!* the set background shifted from blue to red when the game entered the Double Jeopardy! round. Preceding page: Always dapper, Alex has charmed audiences with his smooth hosting style.

ACTORS

HE CALLED HIS 1992 AUTOBIOGRAPHY "WHAT'S IT ALL ABOUT?"

AMERICAN HISTORY

IN 1919 HE BECAME THE FIRST GENERAL OF THE ARMIES OF THE U.S.

✓ HIGH I.Q.
✓ WITTY
✓ TEAM PLAYER
✓ THE PATIENCE OF JOB

BANKS

THIS NEW YORK CITY BANK IS NAMED FOR THE 25TH SECRETARY OF THE TREASURY

It is frequently asked of *Jeopardy!* staffers how one gets a job writing for the show. Openings are rare. But when they do occur, a prospective writer must be intelligent enough to do well on the show were he or she a contestant. Then come the category submissions. After that, patience is probably the best virtue.

BESTSELLERS

THE TITLE OF THIS 1987 NOVEL COMES FROM THE BURNING OF VALUABLES IN FLORENCE, ITALY, IN THE 1490S

BRITISH HISTORY

OVER 300 YEARS AFTER HIS 1658 DEATH, HIS HEAD WAS LAID TO REST BY HIS ALMA MATER, A COLLEGE AT CAMBRIDGE

WHO IS MICHAEL CAINE?

Caine had the title role in
Alfie, whose theme song asks,
"What's it all about?"

**WHO WAS
JOHN L. PERSHING?**

**WHAT IS THE CHASE
(MANHATTAN) BANK?**

Salmon P. Chase was secretary
of the treasury under Lincoln.

TIME'S
UP!

**WHAT IS *THE BONFIRE
OF THE VANITIES*?**

The novel was written by
Tom Wolfe, who personally
confirmed this fact for
Jeopardy! writers.

WHO IS OLIVER CROMWELL?

FAMOUS HOMES

THE TICKET OFFICE AT THIS PRESIDENTIAL HOME HANDS OUT DOZENS OF $2 BILLS AS CHANGE EVERY DAY

FAMOUS NAMES

IN 1970 HE MADE HIS FIRST VISIT TO A TENNESSEE CLASSROOM SINCE HIS CONVICTION 45 YEARS EARLIER

WHO IS
THOMAS
JEFFERSO

FAMOUS WOMEN

SHE WAS QUOTED AS SAYING THAT AS A MOTHER, "I MODELED MY BEHAVIOR ON CHIMPS . . . THEY ARE VERY LOVING."

FICTIONAL TRANSPORTATION

IT'S 70 METERS LONG, POWERED BY ELECTRICITY, DISPLACES 1500 CUBIC METERS OF WATER, & COST 1,687,000 FRANCS

Players often get caught without finishing their Final Jeopardy! answers. In one instance, the contestant had written "Who is Clint Eastwoo" but failed to receive credit. Answers must be phonetically accurate — and complete — to be considered acceptable.

HOLIDAYS AND OBSERVANCES

THIS HOLIDAY IS THE TOP AVOCADO-EATING DAY OF THE YEAR IN THE U.S.; SUPER BOWL IS SECOND

WHAT IS MONTICELLO?

Monticello was the home of Thomas Jefferson, who appears on the $2 bill.

WHO IS JOHN T. SCOPES?

Scopes was the high school biology teacher prosecuted under Tennessee law for teaching evolution.

WHO IS JANE GOODALL?

WHAT IS THE *NAUTILUS*?

The *Nautilus* was the vessel in Jules Verne's *20,000 Leagues Under the Sea*.

WHAT IS CINCO DE MAYO?

**AT 122 SQUARE MILES,
IT'S EUROPE'S SMALLEST
ISLAND NATION**

LEGENDARY PAIRS

**IN THE LATE 1100S, MONKS
AT GLASTONBURY ABBEY
CLAIMED THEY'D FOUND THE
BODIES OF THIS ROYAL COUPLE**

LITERARY LANDMARKS

**A HOME BUILT IN 1668
AT 54 TURNER ST. IN
SALEM, MASSACHUSETTS,
INSPIRED THIS 1851 NOVEL**

SCIENTIFIC DISCOVERIES

**ITS DISCOVERY WAS
ANNOUNCED ON
MARCH 13, 1930, PERCIVAL
LOWELL'S BIRTHDAY**

SCIENTISTS

**BY HIS OWN ACCOUNT, HE WAS
BORN "IN DIAMOND GROVE,
MISSOURI, ABOUT THE CLOSE
OF THE GREAT CIVIL WAR"**

For years, when there was a technical problem with the game board, host Alex Trebek was known to take off his shoe and throw it at the *Jeopardy!* board in mock disgust. Only the studio audience would see it. Alex still removes his shoe and throws it in the board's direction on occasion.

WHAT IS MALTA?

WHO WERE KING ARTHUR AND QUEEN GUINEVERE?

WHAT IS *THE HOUSE OF THE SEVEN GABLES*?

The House of Seven Gables was written by Nathaniel Hawthorne.

WHAT IS PLUTO?

Astronomer Lowell predicted the discovery of Pluto after postulating its existence and location.

WHO WAS GEORGE WASHINGTON CARVER?

New York cop Frank Spangenberg, who once held the record for most money won in a single week with $102,597, was invited to dinner by Pulitzer Prize–winning author Wendy Wasserstein for correctly remembering her last name in a tenth-anniversary tournament question.

TELEVISION

THIS SERIES NOTED FOR THE HIGHEST-RATED SINGLE EPISODE OF THE '60S HAD A 1993 FILM BASED ON IT

COMMUNICATIONS

THIS FIRST PASSIVE COMMUNICATIONS SATELLITE, LAUNCHED IN 1960, SIMPLY REFLECTED RADIO SIGNALS

MAMMALS

THEY MAKE UP THE SECOND-LARGEST ORDER OF MAMMALS, CHIROPTERA

ORGANIZATIONS

WHEN THIS U.S. ORGANIZATION WAS ESTABLISHED IN 1912, DAISY GORDON BECAME ITS FIRST REGISTERED MEMBER

WORLD LEADERS

IN 1992 HE BECAME THE FIRST FOREIGN HEAD OF STATE TO BE CONVICTED BY A U.S. JURY

?

WHAT IS *THE FUGITIVE*?

WHAT IS *ECHO* (1)?

One of the things that the viewing audience never sees is what host Alex Trebek does during the commercial breaks. He will answer questions from the studio audience and clown around with them. He also poses for a picture with each contestant in between the Jeopardy! and Double Jeopardy! rounds, when he will joke with the players and help put them at ease.

WHAT ARE BATS?

WHAT IS THE GIRL SCOUTS?

Daisy was the niece of Girl Scouts founder Juliette "Daisy" Gordon Low.

me & alex

WHO IS MANUEL NORIEGA?

SEASON 11

1994–1995

NEVER UNDERESTIMATE a military man. That's the message that follows in the wake of H. Norman Schwarzkopf's appearance during Celebrity Week as the Gulf War commander amasses $28,000 for the Boggy Creek Gang charity. His fellow celebrity participants include Stefanie Powers, Jason Alexander, Marilu Henner, Kareem Abdul-Jabbar, Alexandra Paul, David Hyde Pierce, Lou Diamond Phillips, Larry King, Markie Post, and Tony Randall. Meanwhile, on the December 13 episode of *Cheers*, Cliff Clavin (John Ratzenberger) blows $22,000 during Final Jeopardy! and loses. The segment proves to be one of the highest-rated in *Cheers* history. Rachael Schwartz, of the Washington, D.C., area, becomes the first female Tournament of Champions winner. *Jeopardy!* now has 42 million viewers tuning in weekly. It is announced that the show has been renewed across the country by stations, carrying it through the end of the century. The May 1994 issue of *Dartmouth* magazine finds assistant professor of government Thomas M. Nichols referring to *Jeopardy!* as "the SAT of television game shows." And in the prime-time world, *Seinfeld* finds itself atop the list as TV's top-rated series.

**SEASON 11
IN REVIEW**

**Tournament
of Champions
Winner**
Rachael Schwartz
of Arlington, VA:
$100,000

**Biggest
One-Day Winner**
Steve Chernicoff of
Berkeley, CA:
$24,700

**Biggest
Season Winner**
David Siegel of
Beverly Hills, CA:
$86,200

**Number of
Five-Time
Winners**
7

Alex appears as himself on an episode of *Cheers* in which John Ratzenberger's character, Cliff, is a *Jeopardy!* contestant. Preceding page: Alex and the crew pose for a group shot during the show's 11th season.

SHAKESPEARE'S PLAYS

BERLIOZ BASED HIS LAST OPERA, "BEATRICE ET BENEDICT", ON THIS SHAKESPEARE PLAY

AMERICANA

THE PHRASE "GREAT FACES GREAT PLACES" APPEARS ON THIS STATE'S LICENSE PLATES

BALLET CHARACTERS

IN A FAMOUS 1892 BALLET, SHE RULES OVER THE KINGDOM OF SWEETS

A letter once arrived in the producer's office at *Jeopardy!* from a gentleman who wrote that he was "sick and tired of Catholics dominating America." He went on to say that it was "an affront to other religions" that the show devoted an entire category every week to Catholic information. It seems the man thought the category was "Popery" rather than "Potpourri."

BODIES OF WATER

IN THE TIME OF THE ROMAN REPUBLIC, THIS RIVER SEPARATED CISALPINE GAUL FROM ITALY

CLASSICAL MUSIC

THE FIRST 4 NOTES OF THIS 1808 WORK SUPPOSEDLY REPRESENT FATE KNOCKING AT THE DOOR

I'LL TAKE FAMOUS CATHOLICS FOR $300

WHAT IS *MUCH ADO ABOUT NOTHING*?

WHAT IS SOUTH DAKOTA?

Update: In 2000, the general-issue license plate stopped carrying the motto.

WHO IS THE SUGARPLUM FAIRY?

She appeared in Tchaikovsky's *The Nutcracker.*

HMMM

WHAT IS THE RUBICON?

WHAT IS BEETHOVEN'S FIFTH SYMPHONY?

CLASSIC TV

SITCOM WHOSE TITLE CHARACTER WAS BORN IN BAGHDAD IN 64 B.C.

ENGLISH LITERATURE

THOUGH NOT NAMED IN THE TITLE, OLIVER MELLORS IS THE TITLE CHARACTER OF THIS 1928 NOVEL

EUROPEAN GEOGRAPHY

IT HAS THE SHORTEST COASTLINE OF ANY INDEPENDENT COUNTRY, 3.49 MILES

YES?

FAMOUS AMERICANS

HE DIED JULY 12, 1804, OF A GUNSHOT WOUND RECEIVED AT WEEHAWKEN HEIGHTS, NEW JERSEY

HISTORIC NAMES

IN 1877 HIS REMAINS WERE BURIED AT WEST POINT, WHERE HE HAD GRADUATED LAST IN HIS CLASS

One of the more famed *Jeopardy!* categories — compiled by longtime show writer Kathy Easterling — is entitled "Those Darn Etruscans." It refers to those people who live in the area around Florence, Italy, that's now called Tuscany. A particularly colorful category clue: "Etruscans did this by gazing into sheep entrails, not crystal balls." Correct response: "What was foretelling the future?"

**WHAT IS
I DREAM OF JEANNIE?**

**WHAT IS
LADY CHATTERLEY'S LOVER?**

***Lady Chatterley's Lover*
was written by D. H. Lawrence.**

Some of the more amusing and punny *Jeopardy!* category titles: "I Want To Hold Your Hun," "Bear Foot in the Park," "I Feel Like Such an Idiom," "Mystery Meat," "Here Comes Bahrain Again," "Auld Lang Seinfeld," "A Category About Nothing," "Tenors, Anyone?," "Where There's a Ville," "Robert Frost Bites," and "Kings Named Fred."

WHAT IS MONACO?

**WHO WAS
ALEXANDER HAMILTON?**

**Hamilton was shot by
Aaron Burr in a famous duel.**

WHO IS GEORGE A. CUSTER?

1960S THEATER

IN THE 1966–67 BROADWAY SEASON, THIS PLAYWRIGHT HAD 4 SHOWS RUNNING SIMULTANEOUSLY

THE 1980S

IN 1989 A STATUE CALLED "GODDESS OF DEMOCRACY" WAS ERECTED IN THIS SQUARE

NOVELISTS

IN 1918 HE PROUDLY WROTE TO HIS FAMILY, "I'M THE FIRST AMERICAN WOUNDED IN ITALY"

SCIENTISTS

IN 1928 HE PUBLISHED "INTRODUZIONE ALLA FISICAL ATOMICA," A UNIVERSITY PHYSICS TEXTBOOK

SPORTS

THIS RACE FIRST RUN IN 1903 COVERS 2,500–3,000 MILES AND INCLUDES AT LEAST 1 MOUNTAIN OVER 7,500 FEET

WHO IS NEIL SIMON?

Barefoot in the Park, The Odd Couple, The Star-Spangled Girl, and *Sweet Charity*

WHAT IS TIANANMEN SQUARE?

WHO IS ERNEST HEMINGWAY?

WHO WAS ENRICO FERMI?

WHAT IS THE TOUR DE FRANCE?

SIT...

BEG...

CAPITAL OF BELARUS?

ARCHAEOLOGISTS

**THIS ARCHAEOLOGIST
NAMED HIS CHILDREN
ANDROMACHE & AGAMEMNON**

U.S. CITIES

**THIS FLORIDA CITY WAS
NAMED FOR A MAN BORN
IN TAGASTE, NUMIDIA,
NOVEMBER 13, 354**

THE UNITED NATIONS

**HE WAS THE FIRST
NON-EUROPEAN SECRETARY-
GENERAL OF THE UNITED
NATIONS**

MINSK

THE WESTERN HEMISPHERE

**EXCLUDING THE U.S. AND
CANADA, THESE 2 COUNTRIES
SHARE THE LONGEST
CONTINUOUS BORDER IN THE
WORLD, NEARLY 3,300 MILES**

Every *Jeopardy!* contestant has his or her own unique way of preparing to be on the show. One contestant reported that he spent the weekend reading the world almanac aloud to his dachshund.

WORLD LITERATURE

**THIS 1513 WORK CONCLUDES
WITH "AN EXHORTATION
TO LIBERATE ITALY FROM
THE BARBARIANS"**

While his assortment of suits worn on the show is practically legendary, *Jeopardy!* host Alex Trebek has occasionally been inspired to wear something other than a coat and tie on the show. He has emerged dressed in one of Elvis Presley's actual Las Vegas get-ups and as the Statue of Liberty, among other intriguing outfits.

WHO WAS HENRICH SCHLIEMANN?

Schliemann was the German archaeologist who discovered the ruins of Troy.

WHAT IS ST. AUGUSTINE?

DON'T LAUGH. NEXT WEEK I'LL BE APPEARING AS THE GATEWAY ARCH.

WHO WAS U THANT?

WHAT ARE CHILE AND ARGENTINA?

WHAT IS *THE PRINCE*?

Italian Niccolo Machiavelli wrote *The Prince*.

"EVERYBODY GETS INTO *JEOPARDY!*" is the show's new slogan. And indeed, everybody does. The show branches out all over, becoming an official Olympic sponsor. Comments host Alex Trebek: "It's an honor to be able to help support the U.S. Olympic Team, the Games, and the Olympic Movement." The show holds an Olympic Games tournament, featuring two weeks of special programming in Los Angeles and leading up to the beginning of the Atlanta Summer Olympics in July. The tourney joins contestants from the United States, Belgium, Denmark, Germany, Norway, Russia, Sweden, Turkey, and the United Kingdom. All of the participating countries currently air a *Jeopardy!* version. The tournament is won by Ulf Jensen, a teacher at Uppsala University in Sweden. The show's latest weeklong gathering of celebrities include the likes of David Duchovny, Lynn Redgrave, Stephen King, Jeff Foxworthy, LeVar Burton, Noah Wyle, Bill Maher, and Swoosie Kurtz. Charles Shaughnessy of *The Nanny* fame is the top earner for charity. (*Nanny* star Fran Drescher will later feature a *Jeopardy!* storyline on the show.) As the reach of the Internet expands, *Jeopardy!* launches its own website. Meanwhile, at the movies, *Toy Story* seizes control of the box office. The medical drama *E.R.* is tops on the tube. And if you like to eat M&Ms, you can finally find some blue ones in the mix.

**Tournament
of Champions
Winner**
Ryan Holznagel
of Portland, OR:
$100,000

**College
Championship
Winner**
Shane Whitlock
of University of
Arkansas:
$32,800

**Biggest
Season Winner**
Paul Thompson of
Cheverly, MD:
$72,199

**Number of
Five-Time
Winners**
8

Alex teamed up with *Wheel of Fortune*'s Pat Sajak and Vanna White as the shows became Olympic sponsors in 1996. Preceding page: Alex appeared with Fran Drescher on her sitcom *The Nanny*.

FAMOUS NOVELS

THE FIRST OF THE 7 COMMANDMENTS IN THIS 1945 NOVEL IS "WHATEVER GOES UPON TWO LEGS IS AN ENEMY"

WORLD CAPITALS

IT'S THE EASTERNMOST MAINLAND CAPITAL IN THE AMERICAS

THE OSCARS

HUSBAND & WIFE WHO WERE BOTH NOMINATED FOR PLAYING A MARRIED COUPLE IN A 1966 FILM; ONLY THE WIFE WON

NATURE

IN DECEMBER 1995 COLD WEATHER KILLED MILLIONS OF THESE WINTERING IN MICHOACAN

WOMEN OF SCIENCE

WITH 32, CAROLYN SHOEMAKER HAS DISCOVERED MORE OF THESE THAN ANY OTHER LIVING PERSON

Jeopardy! games are arranged by Senior Producer and Head Writer Gary Johnson according to a color-coded card formula. Blue is the color for academic subjects. Green covers lifestyle areas. Pink signifies a pop culture category. And yellow is wordplay. The first *Jeopardy!* round might feature two blues, two greens, a yellow, and a pink. Double Jeopardy! could find three blues and one apiece of green, yellow, and pink.

WHAT IS *ANIMAL FARM*?

Animal Farm was
written by George Orwell.

WHAT IS BRASILIA?

**WHO ARE ELIZABETH
TAYLOR AND RICHARD
BURTON?**

They were nominated for
the movie *Who's Afraid
of Virginia Woolf?*

**WHAT ARE (MONARCH)
BUTTERFLIES?**

WHAT ARE COMETS?

Her discoveries include the
famous Shoemaker-Levy 9,
discovered with husband
Eugene and David Levy.

FAMOUS NAMES

AS BRITISH AMBASSADOR TO TURKEY HE WAS ALLOWED TO TAKE AWAY "ANY PIECES OF STONE WITH OLD INSCRIPTIONS"

SCIENTISTS

IN 1992 THE ROMAN CATHOLIC CHURCH ADMITTED THAT IT ERRED IN CONDEMNING THIS MAN

HISTORIC AMERICANS

A STATUE OF HIM STANDS AT YALE'S CONNECTICUT HALL; A COPY CAN BE FOUND AT CIA HEADQUARTERS IN VIRGINIA

BUSINESS AND INDUSTRY

SALVAGED FROM A SHIPWRECK IN THE 1850S, THE LUTINE BELL HANGS IN ITS BRITISH HEADQUARTERS

POP SINGERS

ON MARCH 10, 1996, THIS WOMAN PERFORMED A SONG ON THE BALCONY OF BUENOS AIRES' PRESIDENTIAL PALACE

One of the more creative categories ever pulled off by *Jeopardy!* had to be "Dr. Seuss Meets the Bard," in which the clues read as if Dr. Seuss had written Shakespeare. The clue for "What was *The Taming of the Shrew*?" was "Kiss me, Kate, though you're a meanie; now go cook some spaghettini!"

WHO WAS (THOMAS BRUCE) LORD ELGIN?

Many of the stones are now in the British Museum and are known as the Elgin Marbles.

WHO WAS GALILEO (GALILEI)?

WHO WAS NATHAN HALE?

WHAT IS LLOYD'S OF LONDON?

WHO IS MADONNA?

Madonna was filming *Evita* at the time.

FAMOUS WOMEN

OF A FAMOUS 1955 EVENT SHE SAID, "MY ONLY CONCERN WAS TO GET HOME AFTER A HARD DAY'S WORK"

EXPLORERS

FOR MANY YEARS AFTER HIS DEATH IN 1324 HE WAS CONSIDERED THE WORLD'S GREATEST LIAR

COLLEGES AND UNIVERSITIES

THE COLLEGE OF ENGINEERING AT THE UNIVERSITY OF NEVADA, LAS VEGAS, IS NAMED FOR HIM

The *Jeopardy!* production offices are housed in Culver City, California, at the Sony Studios, formerly the MGM Studios. The show is taped on the same stage where the Tarzan films starring Johnny Weissmuller were once shot and where interiors for the 1970s/80s cop series *CHiPs* were filmed.

SECRETARIES OF STATE

HE SAID, "LOOKING FAR OFF INTO THE NORTHWEST, I SEE THE RUSSIAN AS HE BUSILY OCCUPIES HIMSELF. . ."

EXPLORERS

ON MARCH 18, 1912, HE WROTE IN HIS DIARY, "MY RIGHT FOOT HAS GONE, NEARLY ALL THE TOES. . ."

WHO IS ROSA PARKS?

WHO WAS MARCO POLO?

WHO IS HOWARD R. HUGHES?

WHO WAS WILLIAM H. SEWARD?

Seward was the secretary of state who negotiated the purchase of Alaska from Russia.

WHO WAS ROBERT FALCON SCOTT?

This entry was written during his expedition to the South Pole, which cost him his life.

GO GET 'EM!

AUTHORS

HE CREATED HIS MOST FAMOUS CHARACTER IN 1952 AT GOLDENEYE, A HOLIDAY HOME HE BOUGHT IN JAMAICA

BUSINESS & LITERATURE

ON MARCH 24, 1994, THIS STORE HELD A BREAKFAST TO ANNOUNCE THE NEW TRUMAN CAPOTE LITERARY TRUST

PATRIOTIC PLACES

THIS SITE ON THE SCHUYLKILL RIVER WAS NAMED FOR A SMALL IRONWORKS NEARBY

ARTISTS

IN 1914, HIS BROTHER'S REMAINS WERE MOVED FROM HOLLAND TO AUVERS, FRANCE, & BURIED BESIDE HIM

ISLANDS

ALVARO DE MENDANA NAMED THESE PACIFIC ISLANDS BELIEVING THEY PROVIDED GOLD FOR THE JERUSALEM TEMPLE

GOOD LUCK!

The *Jeopardy!* studio seats an audience of 140. Besides tour groups and student groups, it is typically populated by friends and family members of the contestants. When the show goes on remote, audiences have been as large as 6,000 (for example, at Radio City Music Hall). It may go without saying, but no shouting out of answers or gesturing or elaborate communication systems are allowed.

WHO WAS IAN FLEMING?

WHAT IS TIFFANY (& CO.)?

The breakfast was held
on the 40th anniversary of
Capote's contract to write
Breakfast at Tiffany's.

WHAT IS VALLEY FORGE?

**WHO WAS
VINCENT VAN GOGH?**

**WHAT ARE THE
SOLOMON ISLANDS?**

The temple in Jerusalem
was built by King Solomon.

For the April Fool's Day edition of *Jeopardy!* in 1996, *Wheel of Fortune*'s Pat Sajak served as host — the only time somebody other than Alex Trebek has hosted the show. No mention was made on-air of this being the least bit odd — or why Sajak was there at all. Trebek, meanwhile, filled in for Sajak that same night on *Wheel of Fortune*.

A NEW SET GREETS *Jeopardy!* contestants. The show's Production Designer, Naomi Slodki, describes it as looking like "the foyer of a very contemporary library, with wood and sandblasted glass and blue granite." The season is also marked by a pair of Celebrity Jeopardy! competitions. Laura Innes of *E.R.* and Mark McEwen, weatherman and co-anchor of *CBS This Morning*, emerge as the top earners, respectively. As the *Jeopardy!* season comes to an end, meanwhile, the show gets a new producer in Harry Friedman, who continues in his role as the producer of *Jeopardy!*'s sister show, *Wheel of Fortune*. His first order of business: travel to Sweden for *Jeopardy!*'s first-ever tapings in a foreign country. Not such a bad gig. The international tournament is shot on the set of the *Jeopardy!* version in Stockholm, complete with ring-in apparatus that find contestants banging on plungers rather than ringing buzzers. Michael Daunt of Canada wins the international championship. Off the *Jeopardy!* set, everybody seems to be doing the Macarena, and those who aren't are probably watching the films *Independence Day* or *Twister* (or both).

**Biggest
Season Winner**
Kim Worth of
Venice, CA:
$64,000

**College
Championship
Winner**
Craig Barker of
University of
Michigan:
$25,000

**Biggest
One-Day Winner**
Peter Braxton of
Fairfax, VA:
$19,601

**Number of
Five-Time
Winners**
4

Alex greets contestants at the beginning of a game taped on the fourth *Jeopardy!* set, used from season 13 through 18. Preceding page: Competitors in the International Tournament gather with Alex for a photo op.

STATE CAPITALS

IT WAS NAMED FOR BRITAIN'S LAST STUART MONARCH, WHO GAVE THE CITY ITS CHARTER IN 1708

BUSINESS AND INDUSTRY

"AMERICA'S FAVORITE FOOD", A BOOK ABOUT THIS COMPANY, CONTAINS 12 PAGES OF ANDY WARHOL'S ART

GENESIS

THE FINAL WORD IN GENESIS IS THE NAME OF THIS COUNTRY

HISTORIC GEOGRAPHY

THE FORMER KINGDOM OF SAXONY IS NOW LOCATED IN THIS COUNTRY

AUTHORS

IN 1996, 7 YEARS AFTER GIVING UP LAW, HE RETURNED TO A MISSISSIPPI COURTROOM & WON A CASE FOR AN OLD CLIENT

Jeopardy! taped several episodes of the show as part of a trip to Stockholm, Sweden, in 1997. On one show, the category was "Foreign Anatomy." The clue: If a Japanese *isha* (doctor) asks you to stick out your *shita,* he means this." The first response: "What's your behind?" Correct response: "What is your tongue?" Quipped Alex: "It's a long way from your behind."

WHAT IS ANNAPOLIS?

Named for Queen Anne of Great Britain

WHAT IS CAMPBELL SOUP COMPANY?

WHAT IS EGYPT?

"So Joseph died . . . and they embalmed him, and he was put in a coffin in Egypt."

Comedian and actor Jon Lovitz was a little bit confused during his season 13 appearance on the show. The category was "'O' My," and the clue was, "Marine mollusk good at arm to arm to arm to arm to arm to arm to arm combat." Lovitz's tentative answer: "What is an . . . 'O' crab?" (He should have said, "What is an octopus?")

WHAT IS GERMANY?

WHO IS JOHN GRISHAM?

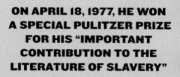

VICE PRESIDENTS

HE WAS THE FIRST REPUBLICAN VICE PRESIDENT

STOCK SYMBOLS

THIS NAME IS THE 4-LETTER STOCK SYMBOL OF GOLDEN BEAR GOLF INC., WHICH WENT PUBLIC IN 1996

THE PULITZER PRIZE

ON APRIL 18, 1977, HE WON A SPECIAL PULITZER PRIZE FOR HIS "IMPORTANT CONTRIBUTION TO THE LITERATURE OF SLAVERY"

FILMS OF THE '30S

1933 FILM INSPIRED BY WILLIAM BURDEN'S 1926 DUTCH EAST INDIES TRIP & CAPTURE OF THE WORLD'S LARGEST LIZARD

BRAND NAMES

COMMON HOUSEHOLD PRODUCT NAMED FOR A 19TH-CENTURY SURGICAL PIONEER

**WHO WAS
HANNIBAL HAMLIN?**

Hamlin served under
Abraham Lincoln during
his first term in office.

WHAT IS JACK?

WHO WAS ALEX HALEY?

Haley is the author of *Roots*.

If you tell the truth, you don't have to remember anything.

WHAT IS *KING KONG*?

The Komodo dragon was
the inspiration for the "K"
name of King Kong.

WHAT IS LISTERINE?

Named for Joseph Lister,
who introduced antiseptic surgery.

POETS

IN 1879 THE CHILDREN OF CAMBRIDGE, MASSACHUSETTS, GAVE HIM AN ARMCHAIR MADE OF CHESTNUT WOOD

SCOTTISH INVENTORS

IN 1815 HE WAS APPOINTED SURVEYOR GENERAL OF ROADS IN BRISTOL, ENGLAND

OSCAR-WINNING FILMS

THIS "BEST PICTURE" OF 1970 WAS BASED IN PART ON THE MEMOIRS OF GENERAL OMAR BRADLEY

MUSICIANS

AS A DISC JOCKEY IN THE 1940S, HE WAS KNOWN AS "THE BLUES BOY FROM BEALE STREET"

RELIGIOUS LEADERS

THE BOYHOOD HOME OF THIS CHURCH FOUNDER STILL STANDS ON STAFFORD ROAD IN PALMYRA, NEW YORK

Alex Trebek has said that his personal hero is writer Mark Twain. He believes that in his writing and speeches, Twain encompassed all of humankind's good points as well as its faults.

**WHO WAS
HENRY WADSWORTH
LONGFELLOW?**

The wood was from a "spreading
chestnut tree," referring to his poem
"The Village Blacksmith."

WHO WAS JOHN MCADAM?

Macadam roads are
named for him.

WHAT IS *PATTON*?

WHO IS B. B. KING?

WHO WAS JOSEPH SMITH?

Smith was the founder of
the Church of Jesus Christ
of the Latter-Day Saints.

BRITISH NOVELS

THIS 1895 NOVEL IS SUBTITLED "AN INVENTION"

U.S. PRESIDENTS

HIS HALF-BROTHER LAWRENCE SERVED IN THE BRITISH NAVY UNDER ADMIRAL EDWARD VERNON

ART

HE SAID HE PAINTED ONE OF HIS MASTERPIECES WITH HIS "BEARD TURNED UP TO HEAVEN"

ANGELS

SLAVES ROWING OFF SOUTH CAROLINA'S COAST OFTEN INVOKED THE HELP OF THIS PATRON ANGEL OF THE JEWS

FAMOUS FAMILIES

CHICAGO'S FIRE ACADEMY WAS BUILT IN 1960 ON THE SITE WHERE THIS FAMILY ONCE LIVED

A partial list of the movies in which *Jeopardy!* has been featured, mentioned, or alluded to includes *Men in Black, Analyze This, Baby Geniuses, The Burbs, Drop Zone, Dying Young, Groundhog Day, Jury Duty, Light of Day, The Peacemaker, Postcards from the Edge, Rain Man, Three Men and a Little Lady, Twilight Zone: The Movie,* and *White Men Can't Jump.*

The device that monitors the electronics of the contestant ring-in buzzers is called the Lockout Verification System, LVS for short, or "Elvis" if you prefer. But the device can't sing "Heartbreak Hotel." Instead, it records — on a VHS tape and computer hard drive — each time a contestant hits his or her button and when he or she is locked out from answering.

**WHAT IS
THE TIME MACHINE?**

The Time Machine was written by **H. G. Wells.**

**WHO IS
GEORGE WASHINGTON?**

The Mount Vernon estate is named for the admiral.

WHO IS MICHELANGELO?

He painted the Sistine Chapel ceiling lying on his back.

UHH,
THANK YA
VERY MUCH.

WHO IS MICHAEL?

The song was "Michael, Row the Boat Ashore."

WHO ARE THE O'LEARYS?

According to legend, Mrs. O'Leary's cow knocked over the lantern that started the great Chicago fire of 1871.

FOR THE FIRST TIME *JEOPARDY!* hits the road with a new specially designed, high-tech, state-of-the-art traveling set. First stop: the Power Players Tournament in Washington, D.C., where the likes of Oliver Stone, Oliver North, Al Franken, Tim Russert, Jack Ford, Catherine Crier, Dee Dee Myers, Andrea Mitchell, Tom Clancy, and Arianna Huffington are among the contestants. During the season, the show also travels to the University of California at Berkeley for the year's college championship. In his new role as *Jeopardy!* Producer, Harry Friedman develops a host of fresh, new categories focusing on current trends, topics, personalities, styles, and fashions. One of those innovations finds the logos of bestselling magazines incorporated with related category headings, with *Jeopardy!* granted access to the editorial staffs of such publications as *Rolling Stone, Seventeen, National Geographic, Scientific American,* and Cliff's Notes. The show has now won 18 Daytime Emmys and stood as the number one–ranked quiz show for well over 600 consecutive weeks. Society, meanwhile, is now being enriched by DVD players, digital cameras, and flavored vodkas. The year's big song is Elton John's tribute to the late Princess Diana, a modified version of his 1987 release "Candle in the Wind." And at the box office, it was all about *Titanic*.

Tournament of Champions Winner
Dan Melia of San Francisco, CA: $100,000

Biggest One-Day Winner
John Skelton of Seattle, WA: $31,000

Teen Tournament Winner
Sahir Islam of Mahopac, NY: $26,300

Number of Five-Time Winners
9

Tim Russert and Arianna Huffington appear in *Jeopardy!'s* Power Players Tournament. Preceding page: During the season 14 College Championship, the stage sported an oversized book with a "punny" title changed daily.

ENTERTAINERS

IN 1997 THIS ENTERTAINER BECAME THE FIRST AMERICAN NAMED AN HONORARY U.S. VETERAN BY CONGRESS

MILITARY NEWS

ON JUNE 11, 1997, THE ARMY DEACTIVATED THE 43RD MOBILE ARMY SURGICAL HOSPITAL, ITS LAST IN THIS COUNTRY

HISTORIC NAMES

IN 1935, AT THE REQUEST OF PRESIDENT MANUEL QUEZON, HE WAS APPOINTED MILITARY ADVISOR TO THE PHILIPPINES

Alex Trebek always has one extra *Jeopardy!* question for each category in reserve just in case the integrity of a clue is inadvertently breached. For instance, every once in a while, when a contestant is jumping around the board, the wrong clue is revealed. When that happens, the tape is stopped, and the extra clue is substituted for the one the contestants have now all seen.

BRITISH ROYALTY

SHE WAS 6 YEARS OLD AND STILL KNOWN BY THE NAME CATALINA WHEN COLUMBUS SET SAIL FOR THE NEW WORLD

U.S. PRESIDENTS

ALTHOUGH HE GRADUATED 64TH OUT OF 112 IN HIS HIGH SCHOOL CLASS OF 1935, HE WAS VOTED "MOST LIKELY TO SUCCEED"

In Case of Emergency

WHO WAS BOB HOPE?

WHAT IS SOUTH KOREA?

WHO WAS
DOUGLAS MACARTHUR?

WHO WAS
CATHERINE OF ARAGON?

The Spanish princess married
Henry VIII, and was known by her
anglicized name Catherine.

WHO WAS JOHN F. KENNEDY?

THE CONSTITUTION

WORD COMPLETING THE LINE "NOR SHALL ANY PERSON BE SUBJECT FOR THE SAME OFFENSE TO BE TWICE PUT IN" THIS

FAMOUS VOYAGES

CAPT. ROBERT FITZROY OF THIS SHIP ARGUED THAT ITS SCIENTIFIC DISCOVERIES SUPPORTED THE BIBLE

20TH-CENTURY POLITICIANS

HE WAS THE FIRST INCUMBENT VICE PRESIDENT TO BE ELECTED PRESIDENT SINCE 1836

HISTORIC GEOGRAPHY

IN 1756 VOLTAIRE SAID OF THIS POLITICAL ENTITY THAT NONE OF THE 3 PARTS OF ITS NAME WAS ACCURATE

The year was 1997. The category was "Before & After." The clue was this: "Hemorrhoid remedy for an old *Baltimore Sun* essayist." The correct response: "What is Preparation H. L. Mencken?"

THE OSCARS

1 OF 2 MEN WHO HAVE BEEN NOMINATED FOR ACTING OSCARS 10 TIMES

WHAT IS "JEOPARDY"?

WHAT WAS THE HMS *BEAGLE*?

Fitzroy was referring to
discoveries made by on-board
naturalist Charles Darwin.

**WHO IS
GEORGE (H. W.) BUSH?**

**WHAT WAS THE HOLY
ROMAN EMPIRE?**

**WHO IS LAURENCE OLIVIER
OR JACK NICHOLSON?**

Update: Nicholson has
since surpassed Olivier.

SPORTS TEAMS

1 OF 2 NAMES SHARED BY BOTH A MAJOR LEAGUE BASEBALL TEAM & AN NFL TEAM

EPITAPHS

THEY'RE THE 3 WORDS FOUND AT THE TOP OF MEL BLANC'S GRAVESTONE

MUSICAL INNOVATORS

ALPHABETICALLY, HE'S THE LAST INDIVIDUAL MEMBER OF THE ROCK & ROLL HALL OF FAME

SCULPTURE

STANDING ON THE BANKS OF THE CONCORD RIVER, IT'S ALSO KNOWN AS THE "STATUE OF THE EMBATTLED FARMER"

BRAND NAMES

FORMULATED IN 1953, ITS FIRST PURPOSE WAS "WATER DISPLACEMENT" TO PREVENT CORROSION ON MISSILES

Nobody who is a contestant on *Jeopardy!* will ever go hungry or thirsty. While waiting for their show to tape, players hanging out in the "green room" are kept well fed and hydrated with pastries, fresh fruit, and a variety of snacks as well as all the coffee, water, juice, and soft drinks they can consume. All this in addition to a full lunch in the middle of the day.

WHAT ARE THE CARDINALS OR THE GIANTS?

WHAT ARE "THAT'S ALL FOLKS"?

Mel Blanc was the voice of Porky Pig.

WHO IS FRANK ZAPPA?

WHAT IS *THE MINUTEMAN*?

WHAT IS WD-40?

THE 1998 TOURNAMENT OF ROSES PARADE

IN THE PARADE LINE-UP, THIS COMPANY'S FLOAT WAS 57TH

AFRICAN WILDLIFE

IT CAN ATTAIN A SPEED OF ABOUT 40 MPH, BUT HAS ONLY 2 TOES ON EACH OF ITS 2 FEET

TOYS

THIS COMPANY'S 4-LTR NAME IS FROM DANISH MEANING "PLAY WELL"; COINCIDENTALLY, IN LATIN IT MEANS "I PUT TOGETHER"

20TH-CENTURY HISTORY

THE NKVD, WHICH LIQUIDATED ITS OWN FIRST 2 CHIEFS IN THE 1930S, DEVELOPED INTO THIS GROUP IN 1954

U.S. RIVERS

THE LARGEST TRIBUTARY OF THE HUDSON, ITS NAME ALSO REFERS TO A HAIRSTYLE

Before going on the show, contestants go through an elaborate process. They get briefed on how to play, sign legal contracts and documents, tape "Hometown Howdies" (on-air promotions for their local markets), sit for make-up, go over their introduction and stories for their interview with host Alex Trebek, and finally don microphones for a rehearsal game before the taping.

A clue about the story of the dog Balto (immortalized in a 1995 animated film) caused a furor among the *Jeopardy!* staff during one college championship. It had to do with Balto's breed. Some sources called Balto one breed, and others described him as something else. It was thought the canine was a Malamute, but the contestant responded that he was a Husky. Even calls to Balto's final resting place could not definitively confirm his breed; therefore, the contestant received the credit.

WHAT IS THE H. J. HEINZ CO.?

WHAT IS AN OSTRICH?

WHAT IS LEGO?

WHAT IS THE KGB?

WHO
AM I?

WHAT
AM I?

WHAT IS THE MOHAWK?

A NEW ERA is inaugurated as *Jeopardy!* introduces the Brain Bus, a 32-foot Winnebago that tours the country in search of contestants through special Brain Bus events. It logs some 21,000 miles per season, visiting 12 different cities annually on its appointed rounds. Host Alex Trebek's status as an icon is permanently cemented (in this case literally) as he is honored with a star on Hollywood's Walk of Fame on Hollywood Boulevard. On the other side of the country, in Boston, *Jeopardy!* reunites past teen tournament competitors in a reunion tournament. The year's College Championship, meanwhile, is played out at the historic Rosemont Theater in Chicago. More than 375,000 games are now played each week at *Jeopardy! Online*. Besides being able to play *Jeopardy!* in board games, on handheld electronics and computer CD-ROMs, and via the Internet, it is soon possible to download the game and play directly on your mobile phone. In sports, St. Louis Cardinals slugger Mark McGwire becomes a future *Jeopardy!* question by obliterating baseball's single-season home run record by cracking 70.

**Tournament
of Champions
Winner**
Dave Abbott of
Cincinnati, OH:
$100,000

**Biggest
One-Day Winner**
Jeff Krause,
stationed in
Sigonella, Italy:
$36,000
($18,000 total
doubled for
Military Week)

**Biggest
Season Winner**
David Bagley of
San Diego, CA:
$56,900

**Number of
Five-Time
Winners**
6

**The Brain Bus
leaves a stop in
Los Angeles.
Preceding page:
Alex took part in
the unveiling of
his star on
Hollywood's
Walk of Fame.**

LITERARY GREATS

HIS LAST PUBLISHED WORK,
AN 1898 POEM, WAS
FIRST ISSUED UNDER HIS
CELL NUMBER

FAMOUS WOMEN

DURING WORLD WAR I THIS
AMERICAN SHOWED OFF HER
TALENTS IN A PLAY CALLED
"THE WESTERN GIRL"

TOYS

WHILE MAKING A TORSION
METER, AN ENGINEER GOT THE
IDEA FOR THIS CLASSIC TOY

RELIGIOUS TERMS

JOHN PAUL II HAS ELIMINATED
THIS POSITION, WHOSE DUTY
WAS TO PRESENT ARGUMENTS
AGAINST SAINTHOOD

EUROPEAN GOVERNMENT

IN OCTOBER 1998 THIS
COUNTRY GOT ITS 56TH GOVT.
SINCE WWII, WITH ITS
FIRST COMMUNIST CABINET
MINISTERS IN 50 YEARS

Change comes slowly to the *Jeopardy!* world. It wasn't until 1998, during the show's 15th season, that the writing staff began working with a new computer database and stopped using typewriters for the primary work on the show. Up until then, the system on *Jeopardy!* had simply been too efficient to mess with, however antiquated.

WHO IS OSCAR WILDE?

WHO WAS ANNIE OAKLEY?

WHAT IS THE SLINKY?

WHAT IS THE DEVIL'S ADVOCATE?

WHAT IS ITALY?

BANDS OF THE '70S

IN BILLING ORDER, THIS QUARTET'S MEMBERS WERE BORN IN LOS ANGELES, DALLAS, BLACKPOOL, AND TORONTO

THE ANIMAL KINGDOM

NEXT TO HUMANS, IT'S THE LAND MAMMAL WITH THE LONGEST LIFESPAN

20TH-CENTURY AMERICANS

ADELA ROGERS ST. JOHNS, WHO WAS HIRED BY THIS MAN IN 1913, REPORTED ON HIS GRANDDAUGHTER'S TRIAL IN 1976

PEOPLE

HE MADE THE COVER OF *LIFE* MAGAZINE 3 TIMES IN FEBRUARY & MARCH OF 1962, & AGAIN IN OCTOBER 1998

TELEVISION

BY SEPTEMBER 1985 "A.M. CHICAGO" HAD BEEN EXPANDED TO AN HOUR & BECAME THIS SHOW; IT'S STILL ON

The *Jeopardy!* Brain Bus has logged in well over 100,000 miles since it went into operation during the 1998–99 season. By the time the 20th season is complete, it will have traveled to more than 60 cities hosting Brain Bus events. The staff doesn't ride with the bus but flies and meets the bus wherever the event happens to be.

WHO ARE CROSBY, STILLS,
NASH, AND YOUNG?

WHAT IS THE ELEPHANT?

WHO WAS WILLIAM
RANDOLPH HEARST?

WHO IS JOHN GLENN?

WHAT IS
THE OPRAH WINFREY SHOW?

U.S. PRESIDENTS

HE WAS THE LAST MAN ELECTED PRESIDENT WHO HAD SERVED AS A U.S. SENATOR

MUSIC

IN 1997 AGNES GROSSMANN TOOK OVER AS THE 1ST WOMAN ARTISTIC DIRECTOR OF THIS GROUP IN ITS 500-YEAR HISTORY

PUBLICATIONS

HENRY NICHOLS' "FOUR SEASONS" ENGRAVING HAS APPEARED ON THE COVER OF THIS PUBLICATION EACH YEAR SINCE 1851

POETS' CORNER

ONE REASON HE IS NOT BURIED IN WESTMINSTER ABBEY IS HIS EPITAPH, WHICH CONCLUDES "CURST BE HE THAT MOVES MY BONES"

FOOD

IN 1929 WILLIAM DREYER & JOSEPH EDY CREATED THIS ICE CREAM FLAVOR, NAMED IN PART TO REFLECT THE TIMES AHEAD

During a "What I've Learned" interview with *Esquire* magazine that appeared in the magazine's April 2003 issue, Alex Trebek comments, "A good education and a kind heart will get you through life in pretty good shape" and "It's just as easy to be nice as it is to be unpleasant, and the rewards are far greater."

WHO WAS
RICHARD M. NIXON?

WHAT IS THE
VIENNA BOYS' CHOIR?

WHAT IS *THE (OLD)
FARMER'S ALMANAC*?

WHO IS
WILLIAM SHAKESPEARE?

WHAT IS ROCKY ROAD?

BUSINESS AND INDUSTRY

IN 1903 MORRIS MICHTOM OF NEW YORK BEGAN MARKETING THESE WITH PRESIDENTIAL PERMISSION

INTERNET BUSINESS

A HOT STOCK IN 1999, THIS INTERNET SITE BEGAN AS A PLACE TO BUY & SELL PEZ DISPENSERS

THE *TITANIC*

THIS MAN, WHOSE INVENTION WAS USED TO SEND FOR HELP, HELD A TICKET FOR THE VOYAGE BUT CHANGED HIS PLANS

STATUES

ITS FACE WAS MODELED AFTER THE FEATURES OF AUGUSTE-CHARLOTTE BARTHOLDI

U.S.A.

IN 1999 SEVERAL COUNTIES AROUND CAPE CANAVERAL, FLORIDA, WERE ASSIGNED THIS NEW TELEPHONE AREA CODE

Actress Jane Seymour was among the celebrity players on *Jeopardy!* during the 15th season when the following clue was read: "Thomas Seymour, brother of this queen, was beheaded for scheming to marry the young Elizabeth I." The correct response: "Who is Jane Seymour?" The namesake actress failed to ring in with a response, noting, "I didn't think you'd do that."

WHAT ARE TEDDY BEARS?

They are named for
Teddy Roosevelt.

WHAT IS EBAY (.COM)?

**WHO WAS
GUGLIELMO MARCONI?**

Inventor of wireless telegraphy

**WHAT IS THE
STATUE OF LIBERTY?**

Auguste-Charlotte was the
mother of Frederic Auguste
Bartholdi, who was the sculptor
of the Statue of Liberty.

WHAT IS 321?

Well over $50 million
has been awarded in
cash and prizes on
Jeopardy! since its
inception in 1984. All
winnings are considered
earned income and are
taxed accordingly.
However, the show does
not automatically deduct
the taxes from winnings;
champions are given the
full amount. They
receive their winnings
approximately 120 days
after the airdate.

1999—2000

EDDIE TIMANUS, THE FIRST BLIND contestant ever to appear on *Jeopardy!*, becomes an overnight sensation as well as a five-time champion. Timanus stands toe-to-toe with his sighted opponents in some of the show's most memorable and inspiring moments. *Jeopardy!* kicks off the season by holding its first-ever Back to School Week, which brings together 15 contestants ages 10, 11, and 12, the youngest players ever to appear on the show. *Jeopardy!* also takes its act on the road to New York City, packing up the traveling set and holding a week of celebrity shows as well as the Teen Tournament competition in Gotham's Madison Square Garden. Andy Richter of *Late Night with Conan O'Brien* is the top celebrity earner, with others including Nathan Lane, Brian Dennehy, James McDaniel, Meredith Vieira, Sandy Duncan, and Jon Stewart. The show also travels to Atlanta for the season's Tournament of Champions and to Seattle for the College Championship at the University of Washington. *Jeopardy!* is now digitally enhanced for interactive television for the first time, allowing viewers to play along in real time on WebTV. Meanwhile, the nation is driven slightly mad with Y2K fear.

Tournament of Champions Winner
Robin Carroll of Marietta, GA:
$100,000

College Championship Winner
Janet Wong of Drew University:
$50,000

Biggest Season Winner
Doug Lach of Columbus, OH:
$85,400

Number of Five-Time Winners
10

Blind contestant Eddie Timanus used a special Braille keyboard to pen his Final Jeopardy! question. Preceding page: The "P" and "A" set pieces part for Alex's entrance.

WORLD LANDMARKS

IN THE 1920S THIS NATION'S CHURCHES POOLED THEIR MONEY & ERECTED A 120-FOOT RELIGIOUS MONUMENT ON A 2,300-FOOT PEAK

TEXTILES

THIS SYNTHETIC MATERIAL IS NAMED FOR THE SPORTS VENUE WHERE IT WAS INSTALLED IN 1966

THEATRE

IN 1999 DEL CLOSE WILLED THIS TO THE GOODMAN THEATRE IN CHICAGO TO BE USED IN ACT 5, SCENE 1 OF "HAMLET"

MEDICAL HISTORY

ANNE MILLER, THE FIRST PERSON WHOSE LIFE WAS SAVED BY THIS DRUG, LIVED 57 MORE YEARS, DYING IN 1999

THE FUNNIES

DEBUTING NOVEMBER 18, 1985, THE CAPTION IN ITS FIRST BOX WAS "SO LONG, POP! I'M OFF TO CHECK MY TIGER TRAP!"

WHAT IS "HEY LOOK AT JACK. HE WON AGAIN!"

Jack Archey was so far ahead in his fifth and final appearance on *Jeopardy!* in 1999 that he decided to have some fun with the Final Jeopardy! answer. Instead of penning the proper response, he wrote, "What is woohoo! Yee ha! Yeah baby!" just to hear host Alex Trebek read it off. Others who were either far ahead or trailing badly have penned similar nonsense phrases or personalized messages.

WHAT IS BRAZIL?

"Christ the Redeemer" sits atop
Mount Corcovado.

WHAT IS ASTROTURF?

It was first installed in
the Houston Astrodome.

WHAT IS HIS SKULL?

The skull is used for the
famous "Alas! Poor Yorick!"
scene. Close was a Second
City comedian.

WHAT IS PENICILLIN?

**WHAT IS *CALVIN
AND HOBBES*?**

20TH-CENTURY NEWSMAKERS

DUE TO POLICE IRREGULARITIES, THIS MAN'S ARIZONA CONVICTION WAS OVERTURNED BY THE U.S. SUPREME COURT IN 1966

FICTION

THIS 1937 MYSTERY WAS WRITTEN AT THE OLD CATARACT HOTEL IN ASWAN

FAMOUS NAMES

***THE LINE KING* IS A FILM ABOUT THIS MAN, WHOSE WORK HAS BEEN IN "THE NEW YORK TIMES" FOR THE LAST 70 YEARS**

FAMOUS WEDDINGS

IN 1998 A 61-YEAR-OLD PIECE OF THIS COUPLE'S WEDDING CAKE SOLD FOR $26,000 AT SOTHEBY'S

OPERA

A 1920S DISCOVERY PROVED THAT SOME OF THE INSTRUMENTS USED IN THIS 1871 OPERA WERE HISTORICALLY ACCURATE

In the 1999 comedy *Analyze This,* the therapist played by Billy Crystal is telling the mob thug portrayed by Robert De Niro that he doesn't think a patient should be drinking. De Niro replies, "That's an interesting fact. I'll have to remember that if I'm ever on *Jeopardy!*"

I'LL DRINK TO THAT.

Eddie Timanus was the show's first blind contestant (in 1999), going on to become a five-time *Jeopardy!* champion and encouraging other disabled contestants to try out for the show. The *USA Today* sportswriter won $69,700 and two cars. What can a blind man do with a couple of cars? As Timanus deadpanned, "I only drive one of them at a time."

WHO IS ERNESTO MIRANDA?

A suspect's notification of rights has come to be known as **Miranda** rights.

WHAT IS *DEATH ON THE NILE*?

The novel was written by Agatha Christie; the hotel overlooks the Nile River.

WHO IS AL HIRSCHFELD?

Famous for his caricatures of theater folk, Hirschfeld's caricature of Alex Trebek was shown on the air after Final Jeopardy!

WHO ARE THE DUKE AND DUCHESS OF WINDSOR?

WHAT IS *AIDA*?

Trumpets found in King Tut's tomb were the same as those Verdi had devised for use in the opera.

WORLD CITIES

AROUND 59 B.C. THE ROMANS
SETTLED WHAT IS NOW THIS
CITY, & GAVE IT A LATIN NAME
THAT MEANS "BLOSSOMING"

DIRECTORS

APPROPRIATELY, THE
100TH ANNIVERSARY OF THIS
DIRECTOR'S BIRTH WAS
ON A FRIDAY THE 13TH —
AUGUST 13, 1999

FAMOUS MIDDLE NAMES

THIS MIDDLE NAME
OF A FAMOUS COMPOSER
MEANS "BELOVED BY GOD"

FAMOUS BALLETS

A MAGIC FEATHER HELPS
SAVE THE LIFE OF PRINCE IVAN
IN THIS STRAVINKSY BALLET
BASED ON RUSSIAN FOLKLORE

THE SUPREME COURT

THESE 2 JUSTICES WHO
GRADUATED AT THE TOP OF
THEIR CLASSES WERE BOTH
FIRST OFFERED JOBS AS
TYPISTS BY TOP LAW FIRMS

WHAT IS FLORENCE?

The Romans called it Florentia.

WHO IS ALFRED HITCHCOCK?

WHAT IS AMADEUS?

The composer referred to is
Wolfgang Amadeus Mozart.

WHAT IS *THE FIREBIRD*?

**WHO ARE RUTH
BADER GINSBURG AND
SANDRA DAY O'CONNOR?**

In the course of researching questions for the show, *Jeopardy!* staffer Suzanne Stone has spoken with 1950s teen idol Fabian, Congresswoman Bella Abzug, and legendary choreographer Agnes DeMille, while writer Michele Silverman received a handwritten fax from author Tom Wolfe. Stone once asked astronaut Neil Armstrong if he got to keep any of those Moon rocks. Armstrong said he didn't.

ACADEMY AWARD HISTORY

THE FIRST AFRICAN-AMERICAN
BEST ACTRESS NOMINEE,
HER LIFE WAS THE SUBJECT
OF A 1999 HBO FILM

SOCIAL SCIENCE

IT'S ESTIMATED THAT OF
6,000 IN THE WORLD TODAY,
HALF WILL VANISH IN THE
NEXT 100 YEARS, INCLUDING
JINGULU & CHAMICURO

SPORTS STARS

BORN IN 1980, THIS
WORLD CHAMPION FIGURE
SKATER WAS NAMED FOR
A BEATLES HIT

HIGHWAYS AND BYWAYS

ON DECEMBER 7, 1995,
THIS STATE OFFICIALLY
RENAMED ITS PORTION OF
INTERSTATE 10 AS THE PEARL
HARBOR MEMORIAL HIGHWAY

THE MAP OF EUROPE

BORDERING ITALY, AUSTRIA,
HUNGARY, & CROATIA, IT'S
ONE OF THE WORLD'S NEWEST
INDEPENDENT COUNTRIES

MOON ROCKS

**WHO IS
DOROTHY DANDRIDGE?**

Jeopardy! uses about 2,700 categories and roughly 14,000 clues on the show per season, with 230 programs taped each year — except in the first season, when there were just 195.

WHAT ARE LANGUAGES?

Jingulu is spoken in Australia; Chamicuro is spoken in Peru.

WHO IS MICHELLE KWAN?

WHAT IS ARIZONA?

The USS *Arizona* was sunk at Pearl Harbor on December 7, 1941.

WHAT IS SLOVENIA?

Slovenia declared its independence from Yugoslavia in 1991.

OLD CLUES

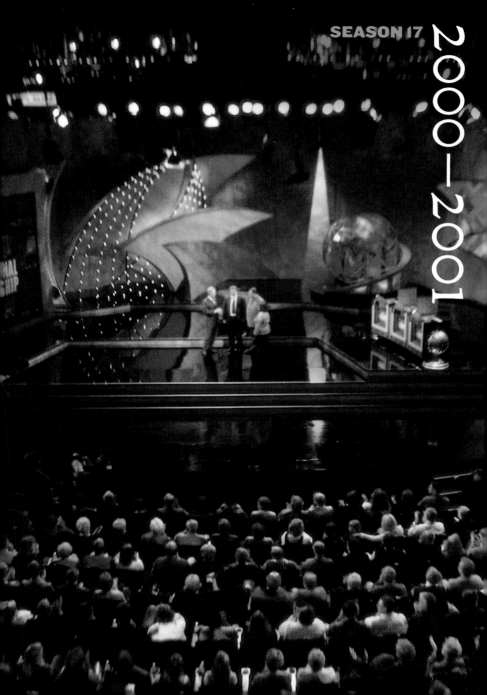

THE QUESTION OF EXACTLY when the old millennium ends and the new one begins is answered by *Jeopardy!* in a Final Jeopardy! clue which read: "Technically, this upcoming date will be the last date of the 20th century." Answer: "What is December 31, 2000?" The U.S. edition of *Jeopardy!* is now broadcast in 30 countries; a dozen others produce their own international editions, including *Svoya Igra* in Russia, *Melech Ha'Trivia* in Israel, *Kuldvillak* in Estonia, *Va Banque* in Poland, and *Izazov!* in Croatia. Las Vegas is the setting for both an International Championship and Celebrity *Jeopardy!* gathering. The countries represented in the international tourney are Denmark, Estonia, Hungary, Russia, Sweden, Turkey, Israel, Poland, and the U.S. It's won by Robin Carroll of Atlanta, Georgia, who has cumulatively now won more than $200,000 in cash. Eric Idle of Monty Python fame is the top celebrity earner; other players include Martha Stewart, Charles Barkley, and Jeff Probst, the host of *Survivor*, the latest rage in primetime, which leads to a boom in reality TV. Scooters make a comeback as a decidedly downscale alternative to bicycling and skateboarding.

Biggest Season Winner
Babu Srinivasan of Houston, TX:
$75,100

International Tournament Winner
Robin Carroll of Marietta, GA:
$50,000

Biggest One-Day Winner
Michael Arnone of New York, NY:
$24,999

Number of Five-Time Winners
13

Jeff Probst, far left, and Charles Barkley, left, competed on the Las Vegas Celebrity Jeopardy! set. Preceding page: Alex took his hosting gig on the road when *Jeopardy!* played the Las Vegas Hilton.

FAMOUS FILMS

HE MADE THE FIRST HOME MOVIE TO BE NAMED TO THE LIBRARY OF CONGRESS' NATIONAL FILM REGISTRY

COLLEGE SPORTS HISTORY

TO PREVENT RIVALS FROM READING ITS HAND SIGNALS, THIS UNIVERSITY IS SAID TO HAVE ORIGINATED THE HUDDLE IN 1892

GREEK AND ROMAN MYTHOLOGY

THE ENGLISH NAMES OF THIS GOD'S 2 COMPANIONS ARE PANIC & FEAR

ROYAL RESIDENCES

THE ONLY PALACES ON U.S. SOIL THAT WERE BUILT FOR MONARCHS ARE FOUND IN THIS STATE

WORD ORIGINS

IRONICALLY, THIS SYNONYM FOR A STUPID PERSON IS BASED ON THE NAME OF 1 OF THE MOST BRILLIANT SCHOLARS OF THE 14TH C.

Growing up, *Jeopardy!* announcer Johnny Gilbert aspired to be a singer. He took vocal training in his native Newport News, Virginia, worked night-clubs on the East Coast, and cut two albums while also releasing three singles of his work. In fact, he hosted a day-time series called *Music Bingo* that ran on ABC from 1958 to '60. This *Name That Tune*–style series sometimes found Johnny himself singing lyrics from songs that contestants would then try to identify.

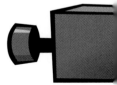

**WHO IS
ABRAHAM ZAPRUDER?**

Zapruder captured the Kennedy
assassination on film in 1963.

Sometimes, contestants who have no idea of the correct answer for Final Jeopardy! decide to at least get creative with their erroneous responses and have some fun with it. One memorably wrote, "Sorry Cory, no Jag." (At that time, five-time champions were awarded a Jaguar.) Another noted, "Who is the guy who's going home with the World Book Encyclopedia?" If you can't beat 'em, then go down with a laugh.

**WHAT IS GALLAUDET
(UNIVERSITY)?**

**WHO IS
MARS (ARES)?**

His companions are his
sons **Phobos** and **Deimos**; the
planet Mars' two moons are
named for them.

WHAT IS HAWAII?

Hawaii's Iolani Palace was built
around 1880; there are also royal
summer residences.

WHAT IS DUNCE?

John Duns Scotus,
philosopher; his followers
were considered hairsplitters
opposed to any change.

TOYS & GAMES

THE WORLD CHAMPION AT THIS GAME GETS $15,140, THE AMOUNT OF MONEY IN IT

FRENCH NOVELISTS

A RELATIVE OF HENRI BERGSON'S WIFE, HE USED BERGSON'S MYSTICAL CONCEPTS OF TIME IN HIS MOST FAMOUS WORK

FAMOUS SHIPS

IN DECEMBER 1620, THIS VESSEL CAME ASHORE AT A SECONDARY DESTINATION BECAUSE OF A SHORTAGE OF BEER

SPORTS NAME ORIGINS

THIS RACKET SPORT TAKES ITS NAME FROM THE COUNTRY HOME OF THE 19TH-CENTURY DUKE OF BEAUFORT

FAMOUS PLACES

IT'S THE TOWN WHERE FRANCISCO MARTO, JACINTA MARTO, & THEIR COUSIN BECAME FAMOUS IN 1917

YOU'VE BEEN A GREAT CROWD. GOODNIGHT!

HA HA HA HA HA HA

WHAT IS MONOPOLY?

WHO IS MARCEL PROUST?

Proust's most famous work is *Remembrance of Things Past*.

WHAT IS THE *MAYFLOWER*?

It was headed for Virginia but landed at Plymouth Rock instead.

OKAY OUR NEXT CONTES...

WHAT IS BADMINTON?

WHAT IS FATIMA (PORTUGAL)?

All three claimed to see the Virgin Mary in Fatima.

During the show's 17th season, a female contestant told Alex Trebek that her boyfriend made a bet with her that she wouldn't say, "Let's cut the chitchat, Alex. I'm not here to make friends. I'm here to make money." Alex pointed out that she had just won the bet.

LIFE & LITERATURE

CUB SCOUTING & MANY
OF ITS TERMS LIKE "AKELA,"
"LAW OF THE PACK," "DEN,"
& "WOLF" WERE INSPIRED
BY THIS BRITISH WORK

FAMOUS AMERICANS

THIS MAN WAS NEARBY
AT THE ASSASSINATIONS OF
3 U.S. PRESIDENTS, ONE OF
WHOM WAS HIS FATHER

BIBLICAL GEOGRAPHY

DURING ABSALOM'S
REBELLION, DAVID TOOK
REFUGE IN THIS REGION
THAT'S EAST OF THE JORDAN
& KNOWN FOR ITS BALM

ORGANIZATIONS

THE PRESIDENT OF THIS
SOCIAL CLUB FOUNDED
BY NEW YORK CITY
ENTERTAINERS IN 1904 IS
CALLED THE ABBOT

CHILDREN'S LITERATURE

3 OF THE COUNTRIES
THAT MAKE UP THIS
LAND ARE GILLIKIN,
WINKIE, & QUADLING

ZIP IT ALEX
AND GET
GOING!

WHAT IS *THE JUNGLE BOOK*?

WHO IS ROBERT (TODD) LINCOLN?

The three were his father, Abraham Lincoln; James Garfield, for whom he'd served as War Secretary; and William McKinley.

WHAT IS GILEAD?

WHAT IS THE FRIARS (CLUB)?

WHAT IS OZ?

The fourth country is the Land of the Munchkins.

20TH-CENTURY PEOPLE

DAVID BEN-GURION DESCRIBED HER AS "THE ONLY MAN IN MY CABINET"

THE MOVIES

THE NIGHT BEFORE THEIR FIRST MASS JUMP IN 1940, PARATROOPERS AT FORT BENNING SAW A WESTERN ABOUT THIS MAN

FINAL RESTING PLACES

THE MONUMENT ON HIS GRAVE IN WOODLAWN CEMETERY, ELMIRA, NY, IS 12' HIGH; IN WATER DEPTH THAT'S 2 FATHOMS

FAMOUS AMERICANS

IN 1982 A STREET OUTSIDE BERLIN'S OLYMPIC STADIUM WAS RENAMED IN HIS HONOR

HISTORIC NAMES

THIS "DRAGON" WAS FIRST FAMOUS FOR RESISTING OTTOMAN DOMINATION OF ROMANIA

Robin Carroll likes to say that she lives in The House That *Jeopardy!* Built. The Marietta, Georgia, resident was a five-time champion on the show as well as winner of the 2000 Tournament of Champions and the 2001 International Tournament. Her total cash winnings were $224,100, which Robin used to purchase the home her family now lives in.

197

WHO IS GOLDA MEIR?

WHO IS GERONIMO?

After the movie, the
paratroopers began shouting
his name during their jumps.

**WHO IS MARK TWAIN
(SAMUEL CLEMENS)?**

The expression "mark twain"
was used for the 12-foot water
depth necessary for riverboats
to pass through a river.

WHO IS JESSE OWENS?

WHO IS DRACULA?

He was born in the Transylvania
region of Romania.

A dedicated horseman, host Alex Trebek owns and manages Creston Farms in central California, which breeds, trains, and provides state-of-the-art care for thoroughbreds. He is also a major wine enthusiast with an extensive collection.

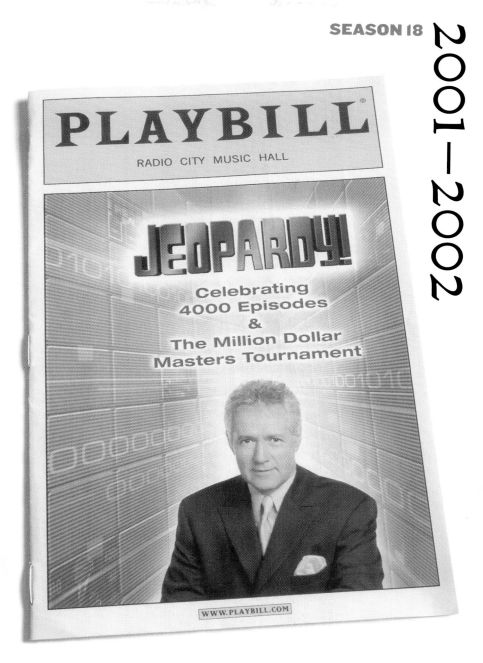

PLAYBILL®

RADIO CITY MUSIC HALL

JEOPARDY!

Celebrating
4000 Episodes
&
The Million Dollar
Masters Tournament

WWW.PLAYBILL.COM

THE MONEY GROWS on *Jeopardy!* as the game board values double, spurring ever-higher contestant windfalls. The show also adds the globetrotting Clue Crew to the mix, with Cheryl Farrell, Sofia Lidskog, Jimmy McGuire, and Sarah Whitcomb selected from nearly 5,000 hopefuls. During their first season, they go in search of clues to the French Quarter in New Orleans, FBI headquarters in Washington, D.C., Alcatraz Island off San Francisco, and cruising the Caribbean, among other locales. The year's College Championship is held at UCLA in Los Angeles and a Million Dollar Masters Tournament takes place inside New York City's famed Radio City Music Hall. The reigning Tournament of Champions winner, Brad Rutter, beats an all-star team of *Jeopardy!* champs to earn the $1 million first prize. Following the tragic events of September 11, *Jeopardy!* commits to help those in need by matching amounts earned by each winning contestant and donating it to the Families of Freedom Scholarship Fund.

Million Dollar Masters Winner
Brad Rutter of Lancaster, PA

Biggest One-Day Winner
Jeff Goldfarb of New York, NY:
$39,999

Biggest Season Winner
Eric Floyd of Athens, GA:
$97,800

Number of Five-Time Winners
3

The Clue Crew was unveiled as (left to right) Sarah Whitcomb, Jimmy McGuire, Cheryl Farrell, and Sofia Lidskog. Preceding page: As part of *Jeopardy!* 's **4000th** show celebration at Radio City Music Hall, a special Playbill was issued.

U.S. STATES

IT'S THE ONLY STATE WHOSE STATE BIRD HAS A MAJOR CITY IN ITS NAME

CONTEMPORARY WOMEN

ACCORDING TO THE "LONDON TIMES", SHE WAS ENGLAND'S HIGHEST-EARNING BRITISH WOMAN IN 2001, FOLLOWED BY QUEEN ELIZABETH II

1980S BUSINESS

IN HIS JOB SINCE 1984, THIS MAN HAS BEEN CALLED "THE PRINCE WHO AWAKENED SLEEPING BEAUTY"

ASTRONOMER'S DICTIONARY

THIS WORD COMES FROM A GREEK PHRASE MEANING "CIRCLE OF ANIMALS"

INTERNATIONAL SPORTS

IT'S THE ONLY COUNTRY TO HOST THE SUMMER OLYMPICS IN NOVEMBER & DECEMBER

When the *Jeopardy!* game board values were doubled in 2001, the highest possible amount a contestant could theoretically win in one day became $566,400. To achieve that, he or she would have to ring in and respond correctly to every clue, hit the Daily Double at the very end of each round, and risk the maximum each time.

WHAT IS MARYLAND?

Maryland's state bird
is the Baltimore oriole.

WHO IS J. K. ROWLING?

Rowling, the creator of
Harry Potter, earned an
estimated $36.2 million
in 2001.

WHO IS MICHAEL EISNER?

Eisner is the Disney chairman
and CEO who reinvigorated
the company in the 1980s.

WHAT IS ZODIAC?

WHAT IS AUSTRALIA?

PULITZER PRIZE-WINNING BOOKS

ONE OF ITS TITLE STUDIES IS SENATOR EDMUND ROSS' 1868 VOTE AGAINST CONVICTING PRESIDENT ANDREW JOHNSON

The *Jeopardy!* Clue Crew, four roving correspondents, spent their first three years on the job traveling to more than 100 cities throughout the U.S. and around the world while searching out clues.

AMERICANA

APPROPRIATELY, THE SALEM WITCH TRIALS MEMORIAL WAS UNVEILED BY THIS PLAYWRIGHT

FROM THE LATIN

DERIVED FROM THE LATIN FOR "TO WALK," THIS WORD IS OFTEN PRINTED BACKWARDS TO BE SEEN IN REAR-VIEW MIRRORS

ARCHITECTURE & SOCIETY

THE TIERED STEEPLE OF ST. BRIDE'S CHURCH IN LONDON INSPIRED THE TRADITIONAL FORM OF THIS FESTIVE ITEM

CLASSICAL MUSIC

THIS ORCHESTRAL INSTRUMENT IS THE FIRST ONE HEARD IN STRAVINSKY'S "ORPHEUS" & THE SECOND HEARD IN LISZT'S "ORPHEUS"

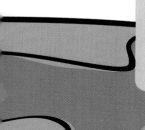

WHAT IS *PROFILES IN COURAGE*?

WHO IS ARTHUR MILLER?

Miller wrote *The Crucible*, a play about the Salem witch trials.

WHAT IS AMBULANCE?

WHAT IS WEDDING CAKE?

WHAT IS THE HARP?

Orpheus is a famous lyre player in Greek mythology.

AW

AMERICAN COMPOSERS

RACHMANINOFF & HEIFETZ WATCHED PAUL WHITEMAN CONDUCT THE 1924 PREMIERE OF A MILESTONE WORK BY THIS COMPOSER

ANIMALS

SCIENTISTS NAMED AN ANTICOAGULANT FOUND IN THE SALIVA OF A SPECIES OF THIS ANIMAL "DRACULIN"

STATE NICKNAME ORIGINS

ONE POPULAR STORY IS THAT MEN OF THIS STATE FOUGHT SO STALWARTLY IT SEEMED THEIR FEET WERE STUCK TO THE GROUND

THE INTERNET

THIS SEARCH ENGINE WAS CO-FOUNDED BY SERGEY BRIN, A MATH MAJOR WHO CHOSE THE NAME TO IMPLY A VAST REACH

SPORTS ON TV

THE HIGHEST-RATED SPORTS PROGRAM IN TV HISTORY, OTHER THAN A SUPER BOWL, TOOK PLACE ON FEBRUARY 23, 1994, IN THIS SPORT

Jeopardy! researcher Mark Gaberman went above and beyond the call of duty during the show's 18th season by including a picture of his newborn son Tom in a clue. The clue: "Alliterative 2-word term for the proverbially soft object seen here." The answer: "What is a baby's bottom?" Tom Gaberman's bare butt went coast to coast on February 26, 2002.

WHO IS GEORGE GERSHWIN?

They watched the premiere of his *Rhapsody in Blue,* which combined jazz and symphonic elements.

WHAT IS THE (VAMPIRE) BAT?

WHAT IS NORTH CAROLINA?

North Carolina is known as the Tar Heel State.

WHAT IS GOOGLE (.COM)?

Google is a variation of googol, 1 followed by 100 zeros.

WHAT IS FIGURE SKATING?

The event featured Nancy Kerrigan and Tonya Harding after Kerrigan had been attacked.

SPORTS STARS

A JULY 2001 NEWSPAPER AD FROM THE U.S. POSTAL SERVICE CONGRATULATING THIS MAN READ "UN, DEUX, TROIS!"

FILM DIRECTORS

IN HIS 1929 FILM "DIE FRAU IM MOND", OR "WOMAN IN THE MOON", HE ORIGINATED THE ROCKET COUNTDOWN

TV & LITERATURE

THE FUGITIVE WAS BASED IN PART ON THIS 1862 NOVEL IN WHICH A DETECTIVE RELENTLESSLY PURSUES THE FUGITIVE HERO

NATIONAL ANTHEMS

"LAND OF TWO RIVERS" IS THE ANTHEM OF THIS COUNTRY, WHOSE HISTORY GOES BACK THOUSANDS OF YEARS

'90S MOVIES

IT WAS BASED ON THE TRUE STORY OF THE 4 NILAND BROTHERS OF TONAWANDA, NEW YORK

The all-time highest money winner on *Jeopardy!* is Brad Rutter of Lancaster, PA, who won $1 million in May 2002 (and $1,155,102 total from all of his appearances). The Final Jeopardy! clue that won him his million-dollar windfall: "He was the only U.S. Vice President elected to the Presidency who served two full terms." The question: "Who was Thomas Jefferson?" Rutter used part of his winnings to purchase a Porsche Boxster S.

**WHO IS
LANCE ARMSTRONG?**

He rode in the Tour de France
for the U.S. Postal team.

It was in 2001 that Alex
Trebek shaved off his
trademark mustache
without warning and
apparently on a whim,
between the fourth and
fifth shows on a taping
day. Why did he do it?
Alex's answer was, "to
make it easier for Will
Ferrell to do his impres-
sion of me on *Saturday
Night Live*."

WHO IS FRITZ LANG?

WHAT IS *LES MISERABLES*?

Les Miserables was
written by Victor Hugo.

KEEP IN
TOUCH!

WHAT IS IRAQ?

Iraq is largely in ancient
Mesopotamia, between the
Tigris and Euphrates rivers.

**WHAT IS
SAVING PRIVATE RYAN?**

The U.S. War Department
ordered Fritz Niland out of combat
when his brothers were killed.

JEOPARDY! IS GRANTED trademark status as "America's Favorite Quiz Show" by the U.S. Patent and Trademark Office. Brian Weikle of Minneapolis sets a new five-day record by hauling in $149,200, breaking a mark that had stood for 13 years. The Clue Crew continues with a second year of making its busy transcontinental rounds, traveling to the Eiffel Tower in Paris, the Colosseum in Rome, Westminster Abbey in England, the Hot Air Balloon Fiesta in Albuquerque, New Mexico, and the Broadway sets of *The Producers, Les Miserables, Cabaret, Hairspray, Rent,* and *Oklahoma!* The year's College Championship, meanwhile, sets up shop at the Ohio State University in Columbus, Ohio. The *Jeopardy!* set is updated with a sleek, sophisticated look featuring upgraded electronics along with gleaming gold, copper, and silver geometric floating panels. For years, teachers have been recommending that their students watch the show and often have created their own version of *Jeopardy!* to encourage pupil participation. To that end this season, Educational Insights premieres *Classroom Jeopardy!,* an electronic version of the show that can be tailored by educators to suit their specific curriculum.

**SEASON 19
IN REVIEW**

**Tournament of
Champions
Winner**
Mark Dawson of
Chamblee, GA:
$250,000

**Biggest
One-Day Winner**
Brian Weikle of
Minneapolis, MN:
$52,000

**Biggest
Season Winner**
Brian Weikle of
Minneapolis, MN:
$149,200

**Number of
Five-Time
Winners**
4

**Alex congratulates
Brian Weikle for
breaking the five-
day earnings record.
Preceding page:
During the 19th
season *Jeopardy!*
debuted a new look
with a new set.**

THE SPACE PROGRAM

IN 1979 NASA OFFICIALS RECEIVED A FINE FOR LITTERING FROM A SMALL TOWN IN THIS COUNTRY

LITERARY INSPIRATIONS

IN 2002, AT AGE 104, GREGORIO FUENTES, AN INSPIRATION FOR THIS TALE, DIED IN THE CUBAN FISHING VILLAGE OF COJIMAR

It was in 2002 that the U.S. Patent and Trademark Office granted *Jeopardy!* trademark status as "America's Favorite Quiz Show." This means that it's officially on the books that the program is the knowledge/trivia choice viewers love most. And it's more than just a slogan. *Jeopardy!* has ranked first in the Nielsen ratings for its genre for more than 1,000 consecutive weeks.

FAMOUS AMERICANS

IN 1920 THIS MAN, GREAT-GRANDSON OF SAUK LEADER BLACK HAWK, BECAME THE FIRST PRESIDENT OF WHAT IS NOW THE NFL

THE HISTORY OF CLIFF'S NOTES

IN 1985 CLIFF'S NOTES' "THE SCARLET LETTER" RETOOK THE TOP-SELLING SPOT; THIS BOOK HAD BRIEFLY REPLACED IT

HISTORIC AMERICANS

HE TURNED DOWN AN APPOINTMENT AS A U.S. SENATOR IN 1875 BECAUSE IT MEANT ACCEPTING A PARDON FOR TREASON

WHAT IS AUSTRALIA?

Parts of Skylab landed
near Esperance, Australia.
The ticket was for $400.

**WHAT IS *THE OLD MAN
AND THE SEA*?**

Fuentes skippered Hemingway's
fishing boat in Cuba for 20 years.

WHO WAS JIM THORPE?

WHAT IS *1984*?

WHO IS JEFFERSON DAVIS?

THE BODY HUMAN

AT ABOUT 63%, THERE ARE MORE ATOMS OF THIS ELEMENT THAN ANY OTHER IN YOUR BODY

FORMER WORLD LEADERS

FILLING OUT HER APPLICATION TO RUN FOR PRESIDENT IN 1986, THIS WIDOWED MOTHER OF 5 LISTED HER OCCUPATION AS HOUSEWIFE

IN THE NEWS

SO FAR, SOME OF ITS MAJOR COMPONENTS ARE ZARYA, UNITY, ZVEZDA, & CANADARM2

20TH-CENTURY WORDS

WALTER CRONKITE SAID IT WAS FIRST USED IN 1952 FOR "NOT EXACTLY A REPORTER, NOT EXACTLY A COMMENTATOR"

THE GLOBE

OF THE MORE THAN A DOZEN COUNTRIES THROUGH WHICH THE EQUATOR PASSES, THIS COUNTRY STRETCHES FARTHEST SOUTH

The doubling of the *Jeopardy!* gameboard dollar values in 2001 didn't result in a new single-week winnings record being set until April 2003, when Brian Weikle of Minneapolis walked away with $149,200 in cash and a brand-new Jaguar. He broke the record set by the highly popular NYPD officer Frank Spangenberg, which had stood for 13 years.

WHAT IS HYDROGEN?

A body is mostly water (H_2O).

WHO IS CORAZON AQUINO?

Aquino was the president of the Philippines and widow of Benigno Aquino.

WHAT IS THE INTERNATIONAL SPACE STATION?

WHAT IS AN ANCHOR(MAN)?

WHAT IS BRAZIL?

HISTORIC OCCASIONS

ON DEC. 1, 1990, PHILIPPE COZETTE & GRAHAM FAGG HAD A HISTORIC HANDSHAKE HERE

OSCAR-WINNING FILMS

THIS 1995 DOUBLE OSCAR WINNER TAKES ITS TITLE FROM A LINE USED BY CLAUDE RAINS IN 1942'S *CASABLANCA*

LEGAL HISTORY

AFTER KILLING HIS WIFE'S LOVER IN WASHINGTON, D.C., IN 1859, REP. DANIEL SICKLES WAS THE 1ST TO CLAIM THIS, A 2-WORD TERM

Blind contestant Eddie Timanus met his wife as a result of his appearances on *Jeopardy!* His now mother-in-law was watching the show and called her daughter to say, "You should see this guy and what he does." After communicating through a game-show chat room, they met, dated, and were soon engaged and married.

CATCHPHRASES

MAIDEN NAME OF AUTHOR EDITH WHARTON, WHOSE SOCIAL-CLIMBING FAMILY MAY HAVE INSPIRED A CATCHPHRASE

THE PRESIDENCY

HE WAS THE FIRST MAN TO BECOME PRESIDENT AS A RESULT OF THE 25TH AMENDMENT

WHAT IS THE CHUNNEL?

The two men shook hands when they broke through the final piece of rock between them.

WHAT IS *THE USUAL SUSPECTS*?

"Major Strasser has been shot. Round up the usual suspects."

WHAT IS TEMPORARY INSANITY?

Sickles shot unarmed Philip Barton Key, son of Francis Scott Key.

WHAT IS JONES?

The catchphrase this led to is "keeping up with the Joneses."

WHO IS GERALD FORD?

HERE'S YOUR SUIT, MR. TREBEK.

ISLAND COUNTRIES

IN 2002 STATE DEPARTMENT SPOKESMAN RICHARD BOUCHER CALLED IT "THE FIRST NATION OF THE NEW MILLENNIUM"

TOP ATHLETES

ON ESPN'S LIST OF THE 50 TOP ATHLETES OF THE 20TH CENTURY, THIS WOMAN IS THE HIGHEST-RANKED FEMALE

PEOPLE

A BRITISH AIRPORT RECENTLY NAMED FOR HIM FEATURES A LOGO WITH THE WORDS "ABOVE US ONLY SKY"

During his 20 years as wardrobe master for Alex Trebek on *Jeopardy!*, Alan Mills (the son of one of music's Mills Brothers) estimates that he's put Alex in more than 500 suits over the years. What's most astonishing is that, according to Mills, the host could still wear suits from the show's first season. "His weight and measurements have stayed exactly the same," Mills says.

CLASSIC LITERATURE

IN THIS 3-PART WORK, THE MAIN CHARACTER ENCOUNTERS NIMROD, ULYSSES, MUHAMMAD, & THOMAS AQUINAS

MODERN-DAY KNIGHTS

AT THE KNIGHTS OF THE GARTER'S CHAPEL, THE HERALDIC CREST REPRESENTING THIS MAN DEPICTS A KIWI WITH AN AXE

MOIST THINGS

WHAT IS EAST TIMOR?

East Timor won its independence from Indonesia.

A SPONGE

WHO IS (MILDRED) "BABE" DIDRIKSON (ZAHARIAS)?

WHO IS JOHN LENNON?

The Liverpool John Lennon Airport used lyrics from Lennon's "Imagine."

LAYER CAKE

WHAT IS *THE DIVINE COMEDY*?

NERVOUS CONTESTANTS

WHO IS SIR EDMUND HILLARY?

Hillary is the New Zealander who conquered Mt. Everest.

In 2002, *Jeopardy!* introduced the category "Moist Things," which had been one of the categories included in David Letterman's comedy bit, "Top 10 Categories That *Jeopardy!* Doesn't Have." It was designed to prove Letterman wrong, host Alex Trebek explained.

OVER 300 GAME SHOWS have now come and gone since *Jeopardy!* premiered in syndication in 1984, including shows in daytime as well as prime time, and on network and cable as well as in syndication. *Jeopardy!* tapes its College Championship at Yale University in New Haven, Connecticut, in October, marking the series's first-ever visit to an Ivy League campus. Later in the season, the show travels to Washington, D.C., for a second Power Players Tournament and a Kids Week. The show's new "Sky's the Limit" setup eliminates the five-appearance restriction on the show for the first time. Early in the season, Sean Ryan, a 31-year-old bartender-student-taxi driver from State College, Pennsylvania, becomes the first six-time winner by racking up $123,797 in his six appearances. The Clue Crew takes its videotaping act to the glaciers outside of Juneau, Alaska; to Graceland in Memphis, Tennessee; to the Indianapolis Motor Speedway in Indiana; to the Berlin Wall; and to the Royal Palace in Madrid, Spain. *Jeopardy!* will have contributed over $3 million to charity by the end of its 20th season. The CBS news magazine *60 Minutes* features *Jeopardy!* in a segment that emphasizes the show's attention to accuracy and security.

SEASON 20 IN REVIEW

First Six-Day Champion
Sean Ryan of State College, PA: $123,797

Biggest Season Winner and Seven-Day Champion
Tom Walsh of Washington, D.C.: $184,900

College Championship Winner
Keith Williams of Middlebury College: $50,000

Over 100 members of *Jeopardy!*'s staff and crew traveled to New Haven, Connecticut, to work on the 2004 College Championship taped on the Yale University campus. Preceding page: Between tapings, Alex answers questions from the studio audience.

FAMOUS LASTS

IT'S WHERE SERGEI
ZALYOTIN SWITCHED OFF
THE LIGHTS ON JUNE 15, 2000

IN THE MEDICINE CABINET

THIS PRODUCT'S WEBSITE
FEATURES CHEMISTRY
EXPERIMENTS LIKE "THE
EFFECT OF TEMPERATURE
ON RATE OF REACTION"

CHARLES LINDBERGH

AFTER LANDING IN PARIS
IN 1927 LINDBERGH FILED
AN EXCLUSIVE REPORT TO
NEWSPAPERS IN 2 CITIES,
NEW YORK & THIS

I KNOW
THAT ONE TOO,
ALEX!

INVENTIONS

ON APRIL 25, 1792, NICOLAS-
JACQUES PELLETIER BECAME
THE FIRST PERSON IN HISTORY
TO HAVE A BAD ENCOUNTER
WITH THIS

LONG-RUNNING TV SHOWS

THE FINAL WORDS UTTERED
ON THIS TV SHOW AFTER 11
SEASONS ON THE AIR WERE
"SORRY, WE'RE CLOSED"

Five days used to be
the maximum allowed
for any *Jeopardy!* cham-
pion before he or she
retired undefeated. A
total number of 151 con-
testants reached this
landmark. But during
the 20th season, the
rules were changed to
remove the appearance
restriction. As long as
players keep winning,
they keep coming back.

WHAT IS (THE) MIR (SPACE STATION)?

WHAT IS ALKA-SELTZER?

WHAT IS ST. LOUIS?

WHAT IS THE GUILLOTINE?

BZZZT

WHAT IS *CHEERS*?

THE PLANETS

IN 1978 ASTRONOMER JAMES CHRISTY NAMED ITS MOON IN HONOR OF HIS WIFE CHARLENE

19TH-CENTURY PHILOSOPHY

THIS 3-WORD QUOTE, ORIGINALLY IN GERMAN, COMES SOON AFTER "WE HAVE KILLED HIM— YOU & I. ALL OF US ARE HIS MURDERERS."

FICTIONAL CHARACTERS

THIS TITLE CHARACTER WAS BASED ON A MAN WHO BRAVELY SERVED THE GUIDES REGIMENT AT THE 1857 SIEGE OF DELHI

THE U.S. NAVY

IT'S THE ONLY U.S. BATTLESHIP EVER TO HAVE A ONE-SYLLABLE NAME

U.S. CURRENCY

IT'S THE ONLY BUILDING TO APPEAR ON 2 CURRENT U.S. BILLS; ONE IS AN INTERIOR VIEW, THE OTHER AN EXTERIOR VIEW

DOES MY BUZZER EVEN WORK??

Many people wonder how Alex Trebek would do were he to play *Jeopardy!* himself — without the correct responses supplied for him, that is. Alex believes: "Against people my own age, I think I could hold my own. Against bright young people with good reflexes, I'd get buried, simply for the reason that as you get older your mind tends to be more selective about the things it's going to remember." For years, Alex has taken the *Jeopardy!* contestant test and always passed.

WHAT IS PLUTO?

Christy chose Charon as a mythological name that honored Charlene (who was known as Char).

WHAT IS "GOD IS DEAD"?

The quote is from Friedrich Nietzsche's *The Gay Science*.

WHO IS GUNGA DIN?

WHAT IS THE *MAINE*?

Battleships are named for states; Maine is the only one-syllable state.

WHAT IS INDEPENDENCE HALL?

The $2 bill has the signing of the Declaration of Independence (interior); the $100 bill has the exterior view.

Which state in the union produces the smartest people? It may be impossible to quantify. But California has produced the highest number of five-time *Jeopardy!* champions by a wide margin, followed by New York, Maryland, and Illinois. Some 22 different states have produced five-timers, with Canada also chipping in six.

LATIN LINGO

FROM THE LATIN FOR "HOW MUCH," IT'S AN INDIVISIBLE PHYSICAL AMOUNT

LITERARY FEMALES

SHE'S THE ONLY FEMALE CHARACTER IN ALL THE A. A. MILNE "WINNIE THE POOH" STORIES

VOYAGERS

IN 1497 THE 4 SHIPS UNDER HIS COMMAND INCLUDED THE BERRIO & THE SAO RAFAEL

THE INTERNET

IT IS NAMED IN HONOR OF A MONTY PYTHON SKETCH THAT USED THE WORD MORE THAN 100 TIMES IN 2-½ MINUTES

MOVIE CHARACTERS

ON THE AFI'S 2003 LISTS OF FAVORITE MOVIE HEROES & VILLAINS OF ALL TIME, THIS CHARACTER APPEARS ON BOTH LISTS

WHAT IS A QUANTUM?

WHO IS KANGA?

WHO IS VASCO DA GAMA?

WHAT IS SPAM (E-MAIL)?

WHAT IS THE TERMINATOR?

THE SUPREME COURT

OF THE 9 CURRENT MEMBERS, THE ONE WHO HAD THE GREATEST AMOUNT OF TIME ELAPSE BETWEEN NOMINATION & OATH

POSTAGE STAMPS

IN HONOR OF THE 400TH ANNIV. OF HIS BIRTH, IN 1964 HE BECAME THE FIRST ENGLISH COMMONER TO APPEAR ON A BRITISH STAMP

AMERICAN WRITERS

IN 1936 THE SAN FRANCISCO NEWS SENT THIS MAN TO INVESTIGATE LIVING CONDITIONS AMONG MIGRANT WORKERS

MYTHOLOGY

THEY WERE THE 2 PARENTS OF A SON WHO ENDED UP HALF MAN, HALF WOMAN

STATE FACTS

AMONG THE INVENTIONS TO COME FROM THIS STATE ARE BISQUICK, ROLLERBLADES & POST-IT NOTES

Jeopardy! contestant coordinator Maggie Speak loves the show's kids' tournaments because of what she hears come out of the contestants' mouths. "Quite often, you'll hear them say, 'I've waited my whole life to play *Jeopardy!*,'" Speak recalls. "I'm thinking, Your whole life? You're only ten! You don't have a whole life yet!"

WHO IS CLARENCE THOMAS?

Sexual harassment
rumors about Thomas
extended the process
to 114 days.

**WHO IS
WILLIAM SHAKESPEARE?**

WHO IS JOHN STEINBECK?

Steinbeck's series of articles
titled "Harvest Gypsies" led
to *The Grapes of Wrath*.

**WHO WERE HERMES
AND APHRODITE?**

WHAT IS MINNESOTA?

THIS IS
JEOPARDY!

How many *Jeopardy!* staff or crew members have been with the show through all of its 20 seasons? Well, of course, host Alex Trebek is one. The others are wardrobe consultant Alan Mills and announcer Johnny Gilbert. It's the first time in recorded history that men are proud to have been "in jeopardy" for two decades.

Do You Have What It Takes?

In order to become a Jeopardy! contestant, hopefuls must first complete a qualifying test with a minimum score. Contestant coordinators travel the country administering these exams, which consist of fifty general-knowledge questions that are very difficult. Check out the following sample test questions to find out whether you could hold your own in the qualifying test.

Tom Walsh was *Jeopardy!*'s **first seven-day champion, winning a record-setting $184,900.**

Adult Test

1. **MODERN THEATRE** *An American Daughter* is a play by this author of *The Heidi Chronicles*

2. **WORLD CAPITALS** It's the capital of Latvia

3. **THE TONY AWARDS** In 1988 he won a Tony for his starring role in *The Phantom of the Opera*

4. **BOOKS OF THE BIBLE** Esther and this daughter-in-law of Naomi both have Old Testament books named for them

5. **U.S. ATHLETES** Her gold medal vault at the 1984 Olympics was a perfect 10

6. **OSCAR WINNERS** Winning in 2000, she called Jon Voight "a great actor, but a better father"

7. **FAMOUS WOMEN** Born in Chicago on October 26, 1947, she's a graduate of Yale Law School

8. **BOOKS AND AUTHORS** *N is for Noose* was the fourteenth of this woman's alphabet murder mystery novels

9. **SHAKESPEARE** Title character who asks, "Shall Banquo's issue ever reign in this kingdom?"

10. **BALLET** The ballet world lost Dame Margot Fonteyn in 1991 and this defector, her famous partner, in 1993

11. **FLEMISH ARTISTS** Like many of his works, his 1630s painting *The Garden of Love* features voluptuous women

12. **ARE YOU GAME?** In bridge, it's a card; in tennis, it's a legal serve a receiver is unable to touch

13. **WORLD RELIGION** A tortoise named Kurma is one of the ten avatars of this Hindu god

14. **OPERA** This composer's *Rigoletto* is based on a play by Victor Hugo

15. **TV SITCOMS** Eric McCormack and Debra Messing play the title pair on this sitcom

16. **ENGLISH LIT.** Catherine Earnshaw is the heroine of this Emily Bronte novel

17. **GOURMET COOKING** Girl's name that follows "crepes" in a famous flambéed dessert made with orange-butter sauce

18. **WORLD FACTS** Since 1888 Easter Island has been governed by this South American country

19. **BLACK AMERICA** In 1896 this scientist became Director of Agriculture at the Tuskegee Institute

20. **BODIES OF WATER** Virginia's Rappahannock River flows into this bay

21. **19TH-CENTURY WOMEN** Because she led hundreds of slaves to freedom, she's called "the Moses of her people"

22. **ROYALTY** In 1993 Albert II succeeded Baudouin I as king of this country

23. **AMERICANA** Cabbage Row in Charleston inspired Catfish Row, the setting for this opera

24. **CROSSWORD CLUES "S"** It precedes beauty, bag, or sickness (8 letters)

25. **MOVIE CLASSICS** Anne Baxter played a ruthless understudy in this 1950 Bette Davis film

26. **FOREIGN CURRENCY** The name of this unit of currency is from the Sanskrit for "coined silver"

27. **U.S. GOVERNMENT** State represented by Orrin Hatch in the U.S. Senate

28. **THE CABINET** The seal of this cabinet department has an anvil on it

29. **FEMALE SINGERS** This "First Lady of Contemporary Christian Music" married Vince Gill in 2000

30. **THE FASHION BUSINESS** Now owned by The Gap, this store originally sold safari clothing

31. **CELEBRITY RHYME TIME** Springsteen's evergreens

32. **MAKE-UP TEST** In 1999 you could apply make-up to Cindy Crawford on the Virtual Faces section of this company's website

33. **NORSE MYTHOLOGY** These fierce, warlike maidens "ride" through the sky, carrying dead heroes to Valhalla

34. **WORLD TRAVEL** Jomo Kenyatta International Airport serves this world capital

Bruce Naegeli took home a grand total of $64,200 during his four appearances on *Jeopardy!*, earning him a place on the over-$50,000 winner list.

Bernard Holloway of Mitchellville, Maryland, took home $50,000 as the winner of the 2002 Teen Tournament.

35. **BEFORE AND AFTER** Russian empress who admires a Fitzgerald title character

36. **ANAGRAMMED MUSICALS** A Rodgers and Hammerstein classic: "Sour Lace"

37. **LITERARY TERMS** The 31-syllable tanka is similar to this 17-syllable Japanese poetic form

38. **WORD ORIGINS** It's the part of a saddle whose name comes from a Latin word for "fruit"

39. **THE PLANETS** They're the two planets closest to our sun

40. **THE HUMAN BODY** This organ fed by the hepatic portal veins weighs about a pound more in men than in women

41. **CURRENT TV** In January 2000 this libidinous HBO show won the Golden Globe for Best Comedy Series

42. **POETS AND POETRY** "The dead tree gives no shelter," wrote this poet in *The Waste Land*

43. **ARCHITECTURE** Concert hall designers study this architectural branch of the science of sound

44. **FROM THE ITALIAN** This term for the text of an opera comes from the Italian for "little book"

45. **ANNUAL EVENTS** Visit France during this month and you'll get to celebrate Bastille Day

46. **COMPOSERS** Sadly, this Polish-French composer had never written a symphony when he died in 1849

47. **VOCABULARY** From the Norwegian for "sloping track," this word is used to describe zigzag skiing

48. **PROVERBS** It's a good thing "you can't make" this "out of a sow's ear"; who'd want to?

49. **MAMMALS** Despite protests, this South American rodent is still bred on ranches for its expensive grayish fur

50. **GAMES** In 1998 this game celebrated its 50th anniversary with a huge game using giant letter tiles

1. **MARK YOUR CALENDAR** It's the month when we celebrate Presidents' Day

2. **CLASSICAL MUSIC** The title characters in this 1936 Prokofiev work are a boy and a lupine creature

3. **GEMS AND JEWELRY** The finest of these gems are a color called Kashmir Blue

4. **THE MOVIES** He's the "boy genius" who starred in a recent animated feature from Nickelodeon

5. **MATH** To figure out the area of a circle, multiply pi times this squared

6. **ACRONYMS** In the word MASER, the letter M can stand for molecular or this

7. **BODIES OF WATER** This Middle Eastern "sea" is the saltiest body of water in the world

8. **ARCHITECTURE** From 1984–89 four pyramids were erected between this museum's Pavilion Denon and Pavilion Richelieu

9. **AMERICAN AUTHORS** He was only 27 when he found fame with his novel *The Call of the Wild*

10. **MUSICALS** Big cats abound in this Tony-winning show that's set in part at Pride Rock

11. **EXPLORERS** In 1518 he convinced the governor of Cuba to let him lead an expedition to Mexico

12. **YOU KNOW WHAT THEY SAY** As Anne Robinson can tell you, "a chain is no stronger than" this

13. **ZOOLOGY** British zoologist J. D. Pye is noted for his work on this mammal's use of echolocation

14. **FIELDS OF STUDY** John Maynard Keynes and Adam Smith are best known for work in this field

15. **SCULPTURE** Tutu much! A bronze ballerina by this artist was auctioned off for $11.9 million in 1996

16. **SHAKESPEAREAN CHARACTERS** Her nurse says of her, "Come Lammas-Eve at night shall she be fourteen"

17. **RHYME TIME** A spectre's sentry station

John Zhang became the 2003 *Jeopardy!* Teen Tournament winner at age 16.

18. **SPORTS** They're Wisconsin's NFL team

19. **FAMOUS NAMES** It's on the record that he's the "father of the phonograph"

20. **ANCIENT LANDS** Around 700 B.C., Achaemenes ruled this land known today as Iran

21. **BIRDS** This tropical bird's colorful, curved bill can account for almost a third of its total length

22. **2001** This former Pennsylvania governor became head of the new Homeland Security Office

23. **CROSSWORD CLUES "W"** Not A.C. but D.C. (10 letters)

24. **WRITERS** This author's books have become movies that include *Cujo* and *Firestarter*

25. **SCIENCE** It's one or more atoms of the same element that vary in atomic weight, like hydrogen and deuterium

26. **SINGERS** This self-confessed "freak" is the leader of Limp Bizkit

27. **POETRY** Elizabeth Barrett Browning's most famous poem begins with this five-word question

28. **TV PEOPLE** Subjects of her high-rated ABC interview specials have included Christopher Reeve and George Clooney

29. **THE LAW** Two-word term for a group of up to twenty-three people who decide whether someone should be indicted

30. **PROVERBS** "Fields have eyes, and woods have" these ("walls have" them, too)

31. **CHARACTERS IN PLAYS** Biff and Happy Loman are characters in this Arthur Miller drama

32. **1999 FILMS** In *Entrapment* she and Sean Connery go after a mask (and it wasn't Zorro's)

33. **THE BIBLE** God told him to speak through his brother Aaron

34. **STATE CAPITALS** This city is the capital of "The Razorback State"

35. **COMMERCIAL SUCCESS** "Put a Smile on Your Face," Vitamin C sings for this chocolate company

36. **AROUND THE EQUATOR** If you live on the equator you'll note you usually have this many hours of daylight a day

37. **MISSING LINKS** Life of the _____ Planner

38. **OPERA TITLE CHARACTERS** He shot an arrow into the air; it hit a guy named Gessler, we know where

39. **PEOPLE IN SPACE FILMS** Freddie Prinze, Jr. was a maverick in this 1999 film based on a popular video-game series

40. **THE CIVIL WAR** Famous nickname of Confederate commander Thomas Jackson

41. **ELECTRICITY** The two basic forms of electricity are static electricity and this type of flow

42. **COMPANIES** The Houston Astros' ballpark was named for this company that made news in 2001

43. **ENGLISH LIT.** In this novel Major the boar convinces the other creatures that man is their enemy and urges them to rebel

44. **FAMOUS QUOTATIONS** A famous 1940 speech by this man includes "...We shall fight in the hills; we shall never surrender"

45. **MUSIC OF 2001** This Lifehouse song was Billboard's No. 1 single of 2001

46. **FIRST LADIES** The first and third U.S. presidents both married widows who had this first name

47. **THE HUMAN BODY** These paired organs in the back of the abdominal cavity regulate water in the body

48. **COMPUTERESE** An island, or a Sun Microsystems web language whose programs are called applets

49. **BALLET** In a famous ballet, a magician brings Christmas toys to kids including this object for Clara

50. **"PH" WORDS** It means love of humankind, or efforts to help humankind with charity

Jennifer Wu of Arkadelphia, Arkansas, brought home the Teen Tournament title and $75,000 in 2004.

Kid Test

1. **FICTIONAL CHARACTERS** He's the headmaster of Hogwarts School of Witchcraft and Wizardry

2. **STATE CAPITALS** Waikiki Beach is a popular tourist spot in this capital city

3. **RECENT FILMS** The Cortez children follow in the footsteps of their secret-agent parents in this film series

4. **LITERATURE** This Greek's fables include "The Hare and the Tortoise" and "The Wolf in Sheep's Clothing"

5. **VOCABULARY** It's a dictionary of synonyms and antonyms

6. **AMERICAN HISTORY** This founding father was the first signer of the Declaration of Independence

7. **TOYS AND GAMES** In chess this piece moves in an L-shape

8. **WEBSITES** Bios of President Bush's pets are on the Kids' section of this building's website

9. **WORLD CITIES** This Egyptian capital is located on both banks of the Nile

10. **ASTRONOMY** This constellation is also called The Twins

11. **U.S. COINS** This fruit is featured on the Georgia state quarter

12. **GEOGRAPHY** In area, it's the world's largest country

13. **TRENDS** Booties the Cat and Zoom the Turtle are two of these Ty collectibles

14. **POP MUSIC HISTORY** Mick Jagger is the lead singer of this group, still going strong after 40 years

15. **FAMOUS FRENCHMEN** This Frenchman gave his name to the raised-dot printing and writing system used by the blind

16. **FOOD** Yankee Doodle stuck a feather in his cap and called it this, a pasta often paired with cheese

17. **MATH PROBLEMS** If you have three dozen donuts and ³⁄₄ of them are chocolate, it's the number of chocolate donuts

18. **HISTORY** This French queen was guillotined on October 16, 1793

19. **CARTOONS** The title character of this show is a fry cook at the Krusty Krab

20. **EXPLORATION** Though born in Portugal, Ferdinand Magellan sailed on behalf of this country in 1519

21. **THE LIVING WORLD** Animals exhale this gas during respiration

22. **ANNUAL EVENTS** The USA's first parade celebrating this holiday took place September 5, 1882

23. **NAMES IN THE NEWS** Once Missouri's governor, he's now the U.S. Attorney General

24. **FEMALE ATHLETES** *Totally Tara* is a book about this ice skater

25. **WORLD LEADERS** In 2001 he was reelected Prime Minister of the United Kingdom

26. **THE ELEMENTS** The name of this element means "water forming"

27. **THE U.S. CONSTITUTION** It's the collective name for the first ten amendments to the U.S. Constitution

28. **MUSICAL INSTRUMENTS** This orchestral giant can have up to 48 strings and measure nearly six feet tall

29. **ARTISTS** He painted *The Last Supper* and *Mona Lisa*

30. **THE DREADED SPELLING CATEGORY** It's how you spell the area in the title of Mister Rogers' TV show

Kids Week record holder Kunle Demuren of Virginia Beach, Virginia, calmly risked thousands on his Daily Doubles. He ultimately earned $49,000 in a single show.

1. Wendy Wasserstein
2. Riga
3. Michael Crawford
4. Ruth
5. Mary Lou Retton
6. Angelina Jolie
7. Hillary Rodham Clinton
8. Sue Grafton
9. *Macbeth*
10. Rudolf Nureyev
11. Peter Paul Rubens
12. Ace
13. Vishnu
14. Verdi
15. *Will and Grace*
16. *Wuthering Heights*
17. Suzette
18. Chile
19. George Washington Carver
20. Chesapeake Bay
21. Harriet Tubman
22. Belgium
23. *Porgy and Bess*
24. Sleeping
25. *All About Eve*
26. Rupee
27. Utah
28. Dept. of Labor
29. Amy Grant
30. Banana Republic
31. Bruce's spruces
32. Revlon
33. Valkyries
34. Nairobi
35. Catherine the Great Gatsby
36. *Carousel*
37. Haiku
38. Pommel
39. Mercury and Venus
40. Liver
41. *Sex and the City*
42. T. S. Eliot
43. Acoustics
44. Libretto
45. July
46. Chopin
47. Slalom
48. Silk purse
49. Chinchilla
50. Scrabble

1. February
2. *Peter and the Wolf*
3. Sapphires
4. Jimmy Neutron
5. Radius
6. Microwave
7. Dead Sea
8. The Louvre
9. Jack London
10. *The Lion King*
11. Hernan(do) Cortéz
12. The Weakest Link
13. Bat
14. Economics
15. Edgar Degas
16. Juliet
17. A ghost post
18. Green Bay Packers
19. Thomas Edison
20. Persia
21. Toucan
22. Tom Ridge
23. Washington
24. Stephen King
25. Isotope
26. Fred Durst
27. "How Do I Love Thee"
28. Barbara Walters
29. Grand jury
30. Ears
31. *Death of a Salesman*
32. Catherine Zeta-Jones
33. Moses
34. Little Rock
35. Hershey's
36. 12
37. Party
38. William Tell
39. *Wing Commander*
40. Stonewall
41. (Electric) current
42. Enron
43. *Animal Farm*
44. Winston Churchill
45. "Hangin' By a Moment"
46. Martha
47. Kidneys
48. Java
49. *The Nutcracker*
50. Philanthropy

1. Albus Dumbledore
2. Honolulu
3. *Spy Kids*
4. Aesop
5. Thesaurus
6. John Hancock
7. Knight (Horse also acceptable)
8. White House
9. Cairo
10. Gemini
11. Peach
12. Russia
13. Beanie Babies
14. Rolling Stones
15. Louis Braille
16. Macaroni
17. 27
18. Marie Antoinette
19. *Spongebob Squarepants*
20. Spain
21. Carbon dioxide (CO_2 also acceptable)
22. Labor Day
23. John Ashcroft
24. Tara Lipinski
25. Tony Blair
26. Hydrogen
27. Bill of Rights
28. Harp
29. Leonardo da Vinci
30. Neighborhood

Jeopardy! 20th Season Cast and Crew

HOST Alex Trebek
EXECUTIVE PRODUCER Harry Friedman
SENIOR PRODUCERS Lisa Finneran,
Rocky Schmidt, Gary Johnson
DIRECTOR Kevin McCarthy
WRITERS Steven Dorfman, Kathy Easterling,
Harry Friedman, Debbie Griffin, Gary Johnson,
Jim Rhine, Michele Silverman, Steve D. Tamerius
EDITORIAL SUPERVISOR Billy Wisse
ANNOUNCER Johnny Gilbert
CLUE CREW Cheryl Farrell, Sofia Lidskog,
Jimmy McGuire, Sarah Whitcomb
ASSOCIATE DIRECTORS Joel D. Charap,
L. David Irete
STAGE MANAGER John Lauderdale
TECHNICAL SUPERVISOR Bob Sofia
PRODUCTION SUPERVISOR Randy Berke
SEGMENT PRODUCER Deb Dittmann
ASSOCIATE SEGMENT PRODUCER Stewart Hoke
ASSOCIATE PRODUCTION SUPERVISOR
June Curtis-Nogosek
SENIOR RESEARCHER Suzanne Stone
RESEARCHERS Lorraine P. Axeman, Sarah Beach,
John Duarte, Ryan Haas
GRAPHICS AND RESEARCH Andrew Price
MATERIAL COORDINATOR Suzanne Jack
PRODUCTION DESIGNER Naomi Slodki
SENIOR CONTESTANT COORDINATOR
Susanne Thurber
CONTESTANT COORDINATORS Glenn Kagan,
Maggie Speak
SEGMENT PRODUCTION SUPERVISOR
Renee Rial-Reynolds
DIRECTOR CLIP CLEARANCE Shelley Ballance
PROMOTION DIRECTORS Rebecca L. Erbstein,
Lisa Dee, Suzy Rosenberg
PUBLICIST Jeff Ritter
PROMOTION MANAGERS Louis Eafalla,
Grant Loud
FIELD PRODUCER Brett Schneider
PRODUCTION COORDINATORS Kelli Hudspeth,
Nakeshia Carroll

PROMOTIONS COORDINATOR Sarah Wallace
SENIOR MARKETING MANAGER
Annette Dimatos-Schwartz
SENIOR PROJECTS MANAGER Annie Crowe
SENIOR PRODUCTION ACCOUNTANT
Christina Gabaig
OFFICE MANAGER Luci Sweron
SPECIAL PROJECTS COORDINATOR
Bill Gaudsmith
CLEARANCE AND LICENSING ADMINISTRATOR
Sean Sasahara
CLIP CLEARANCE AND LICENSING
COORDINATOR Shannon White Lee
CLEARANCE ASSISTANTS Camille Childs,
Holly Arnold, Jennifer Haugland
ASSISTANT PRODUCTION ACCOUNTANT
Reda Smith-Watson
CONTESTANT ASSISTANTS Bob Ettinger,
Tony Pandolfo
PRODUCTION ASSISTANTS Scott Bresler,
Chloe Corwin, Christy Myers
TECHNICAL DIRECTOR John Pritchett
LIGHTING DESIGNER Jeffrey M. Engel
GAFFER Brian McElroy
AUDIO Cole Coonce
CAMERAS Diane Farrell, Marc Hunter,
Randy Gomez, Ray Reynolds, Jeff Schuster,
Mike Tribble
KEY GRIP Luke Lima
PROP MASTER Jeff Schwartz
VIDEO Ross Elliott
GAME BOARD OPERATOR Michele Lee Hampton
VIDEOTAPE EDITORS Kirk Morri, Rocco Zappia Jr.
DEKO OPERATOR Joseph Servillo
WARDROBE Alan Mills
MAKE-UP Cherie Whitaker, Barry Wittman
HAIRDRESSER Renee Ferruggia
MUSIC Steve Kaplan

*Taped at Sony Pictures Studios,
Culver City, California*